STORES DON'T SUCK

STORES DON'T SUCK

THE 5 PRINCIPLES OF AMAZING RETAIL EXECUTION

Melissa Wong and Jeremy Baker

HOUNDSTOOTH
PRESS

STORES DON'T SUCK

The 5 Principles of Amazing Retail Execution

FIRST EDITION

ISBN   978-1-5445-3587-6   *Hardcover*

           978-1-5445-3585-2   *Paperback*

           978-1-5445-3586-9   *Ebook*

CONTENTS

PREFACE

BACK IN EARLY 2020, just as Jeremy and I were putting the finishing touches on our manuscript, we started to hear about COVID-19. Each day, the news got worse. By March, it was clear that COVID-19 was going to be a global pandemic of epic proportions. We knew there would be serious consequences for the retail industry. Sure enough, at the end of March, specialty retailers began furloughing staff and closing their doors, while grocers and essential businesses struggled to keep up with demand.

We put the book aside as we turned our attention to helping retailers get through this period. We provided our resource library to retail brands free of charge, branding it the Covid Hub. This online tool provided store employees with a single source of truth around health and safety regulations. At any time, field employees could find the latest news and instructions, just for their store or district, without having to sift through information that wasn't applicable.

We helped the CEO of a large, privately held grocery brand communicate down to each associate via video through Zipline.

This leader felt it was incredibly important to talk directly to his associates each day, letting them know how appreciative he was of their work and the steps the company was taking to protect them.

We helped a major beauty retailer avoid furloughs when stores closed. They leveraged this time to train field leaders at home. Leveraging our communication principles, HQ was able to notify employees about new training and track their progress, ensuring compliance across the entire team.

A specialty retailer used our communication principles to coordinate a new store opening. While store openings usually require site visits and in-person meetings, with Zipline, all communications and task tracking was done virtually. The store opened on time, just as restrictions were lifted.

A women's clothing brand leveraged our philosophy to communicate with its 8,000 furloughed field employees, allowing them to stay on top of news about openings and create connectedness with a dispersed population of employees. When stores began to reopen, Zipline was the channel used to bring back furloughed employees. Because the brand maintained communication with employees during furlough, they retained and returned an incredibly high percentage of leaders. In fact, they had single-digit turnover during a time when people were leaving retail in droves.

As regulations lifted and nonessential stores began opening up, it was clear that things were not returning to business as usual. Stores took on new roles, and Zipline helped brands organize the fieldwork around major new initiatives like curbside pickup and ship from store.

When we finally had time to pick the book project up again, we realized that even though so much had changed, the principles that we talk about within these pages are still as applicable as ever. In fact, it's these principles that allowed our customers to not only survive COVID-19, but to thrive.

While we hope to never experience another global pandemic, we're confident that this book will unlock the agility and best practices that retailers need to navigate through any challenge thrown their way.

THE STATE OF THE RETAIL INDUSTRY

"WE DON'T HAVE A COMMUNICATION PROBLEM. We have an execution problem."

We hear this all the time from many different retailers, but this time, it came from a company we'll call Arbor & Elm (not their actual name).

> "We create beautiful biweekly newsletters that we send out every other week. Our newsletter includes success stories that are shared throughout the stores—and the look and feel is really what's engaging our stores. We also send out a weekly PDF packet that offers a list of tasks for our managers and employees to do for the week that line up with our brand."

Arbor & Elm has an incredible brand look and feel (they're extremely particular with their fonts and their image, and they even have a living wall inside their office with beautiful plants cascading down—simply gorgeous). Arbor & Elm continued:

> "From a communications perspective, we offer our stores so much support. We give them these beautiful pieces, and then we have weekly conference calls with the district managers and regional directors, who then have calls with their teams. We provide everything on SharePoint."

As Arbor & Elm continued listing what they provided to their stores, we realized they were extremely proud of their work and of their brand. They were proud of the amount of thought, effort, and time they were putting in to create such beautiful pieces of information. And to their credit, they truly were lovely to look at.

What Arbor & Elm failed to realize, however, is that their communications lacked follow through. Their communication packets also looked like a mini catalog full of information—and just like people who flip through catalogs, their store managers and directors were doing the same, picking and choosing what interested them, instead of interpreting the information as instructions.

From a store's perspective, they're receiving too much information: three packets (ahem, catalogs) every two weeks. Are they reading through them from start to finish? This is unclear. Do managers and directors even know that's what they're expected to do? Maybe they get pressed for time and skip a week...or two.

The message corporate thinks they are sending through these catalogs is "these things need to happen." But the way that they're presented is the reason most retailers don't think they have a communication problem—and it's also the reason things fall through the cracks.

We understood why Arbor & Elm didn't think they had a communication problem; they employed a communications team who created stunning catalogs every other week and delivered them to all of their stores. Unfortunately, their communications team spent a ton of time formatting, editing, and making it look beautiful, versus making it more effective.

PROBLEMS THAT PLAGUE OUR INDUSTRY

"The two words information and communication are often used interchangeably, but they signify quite different things. Information is giving out, communication is getting through."

—SYDNEY J. HARRIS

In a time of transition and upheaval in customer expectations and shopping habits due in part to online shopping, retailers have been reinventing their products and brands. Everyone is trying to change the store environment and shopping experience. We all know that store execution is hard. What many don't yet know, however, is that **what gets in the way of store execution is poor communication.** Although companies see store communication as vital, they aren't putting in the time and energy to improve it. **Communication is the train that brings initiatives from**

headquarters into stores, where execution happens. If the track is broken, nothing gets to stores. Most of the retailers we meet with are focused on solving their execution problem, but they are merely focusing on the symptom, not the cause, which is communication.

Communication is the conduit for enabling better brand experiences. Sure, it's not as sexy as a new marketing or advertising campaign, nor is it going to immediately bring new customers or win awards, but it's how brick-and-mortar stores can set themselves apart from their online counterparts. As shoppers turn to online websites for convenience, they also turn to stores for the real-time experience of shopping. They want to smell, touch, experience, and feel the brand in an authentic way. That elevated experience can only happen when store associates are given relevant, correct, and executable direction and information to exceed customer expectations. **If stores can consistently change and adapt to consumer preferences in real time, the brands that are the most agile will win.**

Consistent store execution doesn't happen because headquarters is only packaging information. Like we saw with Arbor & Elm, headquarters thinks they have an execution problem because their stores aren't following the instructions they send out in these beautiful pieces, but really they have a communication problem. Effective communication is about making sure that information is organized, received, *and* understood in an actionable way. Instead, headquarters often think it's not engaging enough, so then their solution is to "make it more fun." But how much more fun can you make it? Just because you spend more time working on "making it more fun" doesn't mean that the stores actually spend more time reading it. The real problem is that there's still some important messages that are getting deprioritized or not getting read at all.

Retailers aren't providing their frontline staff with the tools they need to do their job. Store teams therefore don't have a clear way of understanding what they need to do and why it's so important. They don't have ways to keep track of the work and understand the context behind the message. Many times, stores just didn't get the memo, and headquarters is left guessing how many stores actually did the things they were asked to do.

As companies rebrand to accommodate the constantly evolving state of the industry—online sales, new technology, changing consumer expectations, etc.—they will need to find ways to innovate. Once they do, communication will need to become even more clear and effective in order for stores to carry out the new brand's identity.

Another reason some retailers say they don't have a communication problem is due to what we like to call *tribal knowledge*. In a lot of retail companies, we find *lifers* (employees who have worked for the same company for fifteen, twenty, or thirty years), which you don't often find in tech companies. They've been around for so long that they intuitively understand their part in the big picture, the expectations, the seasons, and all the various systems—they're a part of the company's history and heritage. Unfortunately, since everything has been so engrained, it's difficult to introduce changes. These companies might get push back from their lifers when the business changes because they don't understand the new expectations. And after so many years, changing habits is rough. Relying on lifer knowledge to pass on how things get done is only effective up until a certain point of a company's growth and can be risky given the high turnover. Smaller retailers face a different challenge. Oftentimes they identify magic in the first handful of stores. But once the brand begins opening ten, twenty, or thirty more stores, the store count becomes too large to depend on the original staff's knowledge to guide how things are done.

DELIVERING ON BRAND PROMISE

To compete in today's world of retail, we need to stand out from all the clutter and consistently deliver a clear and compelling brand promise. It's a promise that needs to be delivered seamlessly both online and in-store.

Consumers increasingly want to have a connection to brands locally. The trend has been toward greater personalization of the buying experience and products to meet individual customer needs. Retail is becoming more about the *experience* of the brand and less about purchasing a pair of comfy jeans, a new mattress, or a sixty-two-inch 4K television.

The role of online and in-store buying has shifted, and consumers want (and deserve) a consistent brand experience wherever they are, whether on their computers, mobile phones, or in-store. Because purchases can happen from the comfort of someone's home on a digital device, when customers walk into stores, they want newness and experience. In turn, brick-and-mortar stores also produce a halo effect that drives online sales. A consistent brand promise across all customer touch points is essential.

For example, Restoration Hardware, a high-end furniture retailer, has been making their flagship stores destinations in and of themselves. In their Napa Valley location, an exquisite chandeliered showroom doubles as a restaurant and event venue. Their Chicago store is staged as different rooms of a house they want their customers to essentially drool over. It's an invitation to a leisurely stroll with a glass of wine—and it's a creative way to offer direct participation in the brand. Meanwhile, Walmart, the quintessential big box store, has initiatives in place to transform its brand by making its stores more like community gathering places. Retailers can build a more holistic brand experience by resonating with communities and individuals.

With all of these new challenges surrounding the retail industry, it's a bit unsettling to see that the average for store execution is only 29 percent (this includes high-end brands and best-in-class retailers). If a company is trying to drive a huge marketing campaign and ad buy, but stores aren't following through to reinforce the campaign, the entire effort is compromised and won't reach customers.

Companies therefore need to streamline and personalize messaging to stores, organize information, and put it in context so store teams can understand and deliver on initiatives. By doing so, they'll be able to increase execution to over 90 percent, win customers' hearts, minds, and wallet share, and have confidence that they're delivering on their brand promise.

LEARNING AND ADAPTING

With the immediacy of online retail, shopping has fundamentally changed. Retail brands have been struggling with digital disruption, learning to deal with how to get the right product to the right place at the right time. Companies have also been innovating, utilizing IT and big data to track buying habits and reach customers in more dynamic and faster ways.

In our current digital age, the pace at which things change only adds to the pressure for retailers to develop new products and bring them to market faster. Retailers have noticed how technology-rich companies like Amazon thrive in the new marketplace, and as such, they have tried to adopt some of their strategies. Retailers have embraced data gathering and are piloting innovations in product design and service, for example, to meet the demands of their newest millennial customers. They are also pulling data on customers, taking feedback on social media, pushing out new products, and developing broad marketing campaigns—which we think are exciting as they offer us the ability to grow and adapt to our ever-changing environment.

The following step, then, is to effectively manage internal communications to get directives out from headquarters to the field in a way that helps organize to-dos, enables understanding, and ensures accountability.

THE SOLUTION

Despite all the challenges retailers face today, store execution can be fixed—and the solution is within your grasp. If you set up effective systems of communication and enable your store teams to do their work, you can achieve consistent store execution, implement your brand's strategies, and ultimately transform your customer's in-store experience. We'll show you how in the following pages of this book.

We've spent years working through the challenges of communication and in-store execution, and we care deeply about solving the problems in retail. In our daily work, we partner with retailers to offer solutions, and we want to share that collaborative journey with you.

Melissa spent over a decade in communications at a top Fortune 500 clothing brand, where she helped define the brand and increase market share. It was her stomping ground where she lived many of the store execution and communication challenges and pressures that retailers feel. Through those experiences, she knew there had to be a better way, which fueled her passion to find a solution.

Jeremy's background is in advertising technology and enterprise software. After spending years at Yahoo! focused on product innovation and user behavior, he founded a company that advertises to customers online based on their offline behavior.

Our experiences in execution and communication dovetailed around a new concept of pairing the best technology with the best communication practices to unlock the in-store retail puzzle.

It was a matter of matching up what Jeremy knew about user behavior with what Melissa knew about creating compelling store experiences.

After hundreds of conversations with retailers and thousands of conversations with field employees, we've uncovered five principles that dramatically improve store execution. We're here to share those principles with you and to give you the tools you need to get your organization to the next level. Are you ready? Let's get started!

Chapter 1

CREATE CONDITIONS FOR SUCCESS

DEFINING OR REINVENTING A BRAND and delivering consistent customer experience in every store location can be challenging. We know; we've been there. Sometimes retailers know what elements they have to put in place to be successful but struggle with the best ways to approach and implement their plans. Companies grasp at new initiatives, make last-minute changes to marketing, and do what they can to make business happen.

Before we dive into our five principles of creating conditions for success, we'd like to share the story of how we got here.

MELISSA'S PIVOTAL EXPERIENCE

I worked with a major Fortune 500 clothing retailer—we'll call it Stuff N' Things—during a brand turnaround. Ten years prior, Stuff N' Things had made it big with its fun, kitschy fashion. It was a little bit retro, their marketing exuded off-center humor, and the brand caught people's attention because it was new and different at the time, not to mention incredibly affordable.

Stuff N' Things then went through a couple of brand president changes, and a lot of executive changes. Their commercials and messaging grew outdated, and they no longer had a cohesive story to tell the customer about what they offered. It didn't resonate with people as much as it did in previous years. Stuff N' Things focused too much on what worked for them in the past and not enough on what was currently happening in the industry. Customer preferences and sentiments had evolved, and from a products perspective, the fashion no longer spoke to consumers.

When you go into a store, you have an expectation about the type of product you're going to see. If you go into Armani, for example, you know their offerings will be high end. If you visit Lululemon, you know they offer sportswear. Customers no longer had a feeling for what Stuff N' Things offered. We didn't provide a reason for customers to shop with us.

The organization was not aligned. The marketing was stale. The product was disjointed without a specific point of view. The stores were a mess, too, so the store experience was terrible. They weren't clean. There were clothes piled up in the fitting rooms. Dust bunnies flew across the floor. They just weren't shoppable. The store teams were disengaged, and for good reason: Stuff N' Things didn't give them a reason to believe. Internally, no one knew what the priorities were, and because no one was aligned, sales dropped year after year.

Then, a new president came in and started turning things around. From all parts of the business, we started to reinvent what the brand meant. We started with redefining who our target customer was. Who did we want shopping in our stores? What was she buying? Who was she buying it for? What did she look like? What was her average income?

From the product perspective, what type of product did this customer want? What did she wear in her day-to-day life? What did her family wear? What were her priorities? What social media feeds did she look at? Stuff N' Things started looking at their product assortments through glasses that answered the question "Why should she shop from us?"

From a marketing perspective, they looked at how to keep the spirit of Stuff N' Things—the fun, irreverent twinkle that the brand had built—but make it more modern so it resonated with a younger demographic. Marketing started looking at the imagery, the messaging, the channels that we were communicating from—all centered around this target customer.

My role at the time was store communication and operations, and we were tasked with improving the store experience. From the store perspective, we needed to figure out what type of experience we wanted this target customer to have when she'd walk through our doors. If she was a mom with kids and a family, she was pressed for time, so she needed to find what she was looking for quickly. She wanted to see what she could buy for her family and what outfits matched together in an easy, accessible way. She didn't have time to piece outfits together. We needed to help her make those decisions. That also meant the shelves needed to be restocked, associates needed to be friendly, not overbearing, and the stores needed to be clean.

The challenge was creating this store experience consistently across Stuff N' Things' 1,200 stores and roughly 20,000 store employees. How do I tell them what they're expected to do to help turn the brand around? How do I explain the roles in making that happen? How do I give them a reason to believe?

That's all communication. And I needed to tell them in a way that made sense and that would excite them about helping move the brand to a more aspirational place.

Inconsistent Store Execution

I learned early on, as many retail leaders do, that even though we'd identified our new target customer and started marketing toward her, execution in stores was still inconsistent. Stuff N' Things' marketing team put out tongue-in-cheek commercials and ad campaigns that were fun and engaging, but when headquarters visited stores, they'd find that the marketing image and brand identity did not match, that the initiatives the stores were supposed to implement were not executed. Displays hadn't been changed, merchandise hadn't been moved, and overstocked inventory hadn't been relocated to the front of the store. Headquarters had been working their tails off to rebrand Stuff N' Things and to give a reason for customers to shop again, and to find out that the train broke down at the last mile with store execution was disheartening—not to mention frustrating.

Needless to say, they were not happy. And oh, I heard about it.

It turned out less than about 20 percent of stores were following the strategic initiatives that would turn the brand's look and feel around. When I reached out to the stores that didn't implement the instructions, time and time again store managers would offer the same explanation: "we didn't get the memo," or "I didn't see the direction." After digging a bit deeper, the lack of execution of initiatives always pointed back to imprecise messaging, too many things to focus on, too many places to go for direction, and not enough resources to make it happen.

In other words, it always came down to unclear communication. As a result, I was asked to conduct a store communication assessment and evolution. The goals were to have more control in stores, engage associates, and increase sales. But the problem was that we didn't have the right tools to do it.

I spent years of my life and an exorbitant amount of energy—not to mention drinking perhaps a bit too much wine—trying to figure it all out (let's be honest: there's never enough wine!). We held focus groups and I spoke with thousands of staff members in stores, upper field, and headquarters about what they thought worked and what didn't. I traveled with district managers to see how they managed their teams, asking them what their pain points were concerning communication. How can the corporate office help you do a better job? What can we create that would make it easier for you to execute? Where do you go to get the information you need to run your business? Is it through text? Is it through a district manager? Is it through email?

I spent a lot of time with store managers, because there are various roles within the store. A store could have up to thirty people working, so I needed to know what information was relevant to them. How did they work? How did they communicate and delegate priorities among their team? I focused on timing too. When did stores want to receive communication so that they could plan appropriately? How did they want to receive the information? What was the gulp rate of information? How could we engage them and help them understand where we're heading as an organization? How do I get store associates to believe in the changes and their role in bringing them to life?

At headquarters, we talked about the back-end processes that were impeding us from getting the right information to stores quickly and effectively. We talked about communication channels. Communications leaders told me they were sending pages upon pages of directions describing specific tasks. One event could have fifteen different to-dos, and stores would receive instructions for a dozen different events. Most retailers were either emailing stores, using antiquated systems, posting on SharePoint, or creating weekly newsletters. Some even faxed!

It was a process of figuring out how to communicate better, execute faster, and how to get store teams to deliver on the brand promise more effectively. I came to see that everyone cared about the brand and their role in the company, but they weren't equipped with the information they needed to do their best job. I also learned that if frontline staff received the right information through message-appropriate communication channels, they could deliver on the promise of the brand. It wasn't a problem of apathy or poor hires. It was a matter of empowering staff with the right direction, context, and clarity about the product, and how they could effectively promote the brand.

I was passionate about finding solutions. Those years were my education, and Stuff N' Things was my lab. My job became my research bed for solving the long-standing problems I encountered. To benchmark best practices, I even extended my research across the retail industry. I engaged with retailers from other companies and networked broadly—and I learned that we weren't alone. Other retailers also faced similar communications and execution struggles.

After seeing consistent themes crop up again and again, I knew everyone was facing similar problems. Ineffective communication was preventing execution, we didn't have the technology to enable headquarters to engage with stores in more dynamic ways, and there wasn't an easy way for store teams to keep track of work or engage with the brand. It became increasingly apparent that when a company needed to market a new product or reposition its brand, it needed its field staff to know their role and the part they played in messaging and sales. This required a leadership philosophy of being in service to stores and listening to what people needed in order to get the job done better. Companies needed to know what's working and what's not. It also became apparent that leaders needed to listen to their frontlines and commit to empowering their staff.

Starting at the Top

When I fully understood the problem, I knew that improvements required organizational buy-in, meaning I had to get executive endorsement and alignment across the company.

I printed out all the communications Stuff N' Things sent during one month, and it came to five hundred pages. I created visuals to show executives the volume of messaging to store managers and then took them through the communication journey of what it took to roll out an initiative to stores. When they fully understood the communication and execution problem, they were on board and embraced a mindset of being in service to clearing up communications so that people could do better work.

I was pulled off other projects and assigned to solving this major problem. I engaged store managers, and we took a hard look at what was effective and what wasn't, which practices to keep and which needed to change, and what behaviors worked best for store managers. How effective were our email communications or our loss prevention practices at the end of the week? Where were we struggling and what needed to change in order to make it easier for people to do their jobs?

We found that everyone's role along the value chain—from headquarters to regional directors, district managers to store managers and staff—needed to be optimized. Execution doesn't work if it's not easy for everyone, and one sticking point along the chain can hinder the entire system.

In the past, Stuff N' Things sent communications to remind stores of what they needed to do on certain days. But it took thirty minutes of cutting and pasting to put out one message, and there'd be eighty left to go—clearly not an efficient operation. We needed to find the path of least resistance. Store managers needed to know the most essential information, such as when an event started and when a task was due, without all the clutter. They also needed to know which messages applied directly to them. We often found disconnects between store managers, regional and district managers, and headquarters.

Every retailer is familiar with the sheer volume of miscommunication and lack of coherence that can upset store operations such as displays that make product unattractive, with clothes piled high on tables and outmoded style choices. Poor or misunderstood messaging leads to execution errors that directly impact customer experience and distort brand perception.

Ineffective messaging means everyone is losing. I knew there had to be a better way, and I knew it would require technological innovation, which is where Jeremy came into the picture. Jeremy came out of the new world of advertising technology, where he founded a company that helped retailers with what is called *retargeting*.

HOW JEREMY JOINED TO HELP

My work involved targeting online ads to potential buyers who had shopped in a company's retail stores. One of the things we focused on was how to affect customer behavior. How can a retailer drive a customer to their store?

Online, we have the ability to track all the metrics and behaviors that contribute to a successful sale. As a software engineer and business analyst, I've spent more than twenty years looking at processes and finding ways to make them more efficient. My work has always been focused on the human aspect of technology and how behavior can be affected with simple nudges in new directions.

My objectives have been to build new advertising systems that achieve awesome results through extremely targeted behavior campaigns. I came to realize that everyone is competing for the same advertising spend, and that the companies who win are the ones that are able to convert customers at the highest rate.

In the online world, there are thousands of tools for testing and iterating on the ability to convert a customer. But in brick-and-mortar stores, retailers still rely on constant in-person visits, foot traffic counters, and sales numbers. Almost three-quarters of retailers guess their store execution rate, and the median store execution rate is only 29 percent. You simply can't know what's working with this level of execution—and it's getting worse, not better.

Melissa's insight into the industry helped me understand why. In our conversations, I realized that brick-and-mortar retailers didn't have the ability to track the relationship between their communications to stores and the execution rate at each store. They couldn't measure how they might improve their execution.

The question was how to set up a system and infrastructure to channel the most effective communications, especially since it had become a bottleneck to fast and accurate execution.

What was needed was a culture of change, so the two of us partnered to bring sorely needed transformational change to the retail communications chain. We applied our combined research with leading-edge technology to refine a system of five principles.

With Stuff N' Things, Melissa was able to implement the first four principles, but she wasn't able to provide a feedback loop on execution, which is something she knew was important to retailers wanting to know whether their stores put up their signs or not, for example. With Melissa's insight into the industry, and my experience in technology, we created Zipline to offer retailers specifically designed technology to suit their needs.

At Stuff N' Things, and with the final implementation of Zipline, we succeeded. We not only gave store teams a reason to believe, but they became proud of the brand, which translated into proper execution across all the stores. That final mile of work came through. Stuff N' Things' store experience improved dramatically, and it gave people a reason to shop again. As a result, Stuff N' Things led its brand's success. It was the most financially successful of its five brands.

A 2015 Fortune article reported that the Stuff N' Things had reversed a trend of declines, and had increased annual sales by $1 billion over four years.

THE FIVE PRINCIPLES

We specifically designed the five principles for highly effective communications and execution. Each principle is a step on the way to creating a fully integrated system of messaging, motivating, and engaging store teams. Functionally, they stack together, one upon the other for achieving the best retail experience.

The steps follow a sequential order for mastering the entire framework, so don't skip ahead or pick and choose! The order is important. In our experience, when organizations try to leapfrog the steps, they often fail. When the framework is broken, the whole process can derail quickly. You'll see why as you begin to explore and apply the principles in their specific order.

Principle 1: Create an Aligned Organization

Creating aligned organizations is about making sure that everyone knows what their role is along the chain of communication and execution. An organization is an ecosystem. Creating an aligned organization requires building and nurturing a well-oiled machine. It's never scattershot. Unaligned companies generate a lot of spin and confusion.

An aligned organization looks more like a performance at Cirque du Soleil. Everyone knows their part. Everyone knows the timing, and expectations are clear. When an organization is aligned, everything works quicker and more efficiently.

Principle 2: Create Intent-Based Communication Channels

Retailers often use a mixed bag of communication tools with no coherent plan. Using the right tool for the job is critical for effective execution. Intent-based communication channels look at the types of communication tools retailers use to effectively communicate.

The medium you chose should define the message. Therefore,

communication channels need to be chosen carefully and deliberatively, according to the content and purpose of the message.

Principle 3: Send the Right Message at the Right Time

We live and work in an age of real-time communication. Information technology allows retailers to convey information to stores in the moment, which is extremely important with how quickly things can change. Creating and sending catalogs—as beautiful as they might be—are a thing of the past. Let them go. Instead, messages need to be sent in more digestible pieces. The principle of sending the right message at the right time uses technology to break the old calcification of messaging.

Principle 4: Empower Your Workforce

Effective communication gives meaning to work. Empowering your workforce requires engaging people at all levels. When people know the why and the context of what is being communicated, they are more engaged, inspired, and empowered to execute their work. Staff need to know why an individual task is important in the larger picture and why their role is critical. They need to see how the actions they'll be taking for an initiative will impact the result. We need to give them a reason to believe.

An important note about empowerment goes back to what we said earlier about how the five principles follow a sequential order. Empowering employees may seem like the easiest step, so leaders sometimes start with this one—which is a big mistake.

When a workforce is empowered without a strong foundation and operational layer, it results in a lot of in-store chaos and confusion. In other words, store staff can be empowered to go rogue.

So remember: the five principles work best when applied in the correct order.

Principle 5: Measure the Execution

In order for your business to move forward and evaluate the effectiveness of its initiatives, you need to be able to measure your success. You need to see how effective your programs have been and whether or not your investments have been worth it. Measuring the success of execution gets everyone on the same page of accountability. It's the feedback loop that provides the measurable data needed to make any necessary adjustments as you move forward.

The first four principles lay the groundwork for enabling a company to measure the impact of their communications and execution, whereas the last one pulls everything together. Principle five is the keystone step of the whole system, and it's necessary for building a more responsive and effective organization. When you analyze your data and measure your success, you can figure out if your alignment is off or if your workforce empowerment is effective enough.

In the following pages, we take a deeper look into the five principles and how they can help your company become a more effective retail organization.

Chapter 2

PRINCIPLE 1:
CREATE AN ALIGNED
ORGANIZATION

IT WAS THE BEGINNING OF DECEMBER, right before a weekend, and the CEO of Fashionistas (not the retailer's real name) came up with a brilliant Christmas promotion that would drive sales across all of his one thousand stores. It included Santa Claus and reindeer to attract families to shop, and sales and deals for young, single people. The CEO shared his promotion idea with his team at headquarters, claiming it would beat last year's sales record, and told them to share the promotion with the stores.

Everyone at headquarters started to scramble to figure out how to make it happen. Things moved quickly as people across departments prepared instructions to be sent to each store. When double-checking the plan, the communications executive

discovered he had different information than the marketing executive in regards to which stores would receive which instructions.

"Which meeting were you in? Was it the 3 p.m. meeting?"

"No, I was at the 2 p.m. meeting. Who was in that meeting?
Was the CEO at the 3 p.m. one?"

Alignment among departments, even at this early stage,
already began to falter. After spending some time checking to
see which executive had it right, they confirmed that the promotion would be different for low-volume stores than for the
high-volume ones. The promotion finally came into focus, and
they solidified all the details for proper store execution. They
handed the directives off to the communications team, who then
packed and sent them out to the one thousand stores.

Phew! Everyone at headquarters was stoked; their job was
done. They were proud of their hustle, and thought the promotion
would be a success. A celebration was in order!

Meanwhile, upon reading the instructions, one small-town
American store mistakenly thought they were a high-volume store
instead of a low-volume store, so they executed the high-volume
store promotion. Since the communication was sent directly to
the stores, when the regional manager visited, he confirmed the
promotion was set up, but he didn't know it was the wrong one.
During his visit, everything seemed to be going fine, just fine.

The weekend came to a close, but Monday morning reads
revealed that business was down across stores. The promotion
wasn't tracking as expected.

Uh oh.

Headquarters started to scramble again. They needed to make

changes to the promotion to make up for lost sales. Visual started testing different displays, trying to figure out what outfitting would work best. They also looked at merchandising displays. Would lighting make a difference? Should we show kids' clothes? Marketing started testing different signage. Did green resonate better than red? Did this elf grab someone's interest more than these boxes of presents?

Pricing looked at the different product categories, like girls' fleeced hoodies or men's pajama pants. They not only started maniacally looking at the price points for broader categories like sweaters, but also to individual styles of the assortment.

After a few hectic hours, the departments at headquarters solidified their changes to the promotion, and by that afternoon, they had the communications team send their updated instructions to all the stores.

Because the update was sent midday, the stores on the East Coast missed it because of the time difference. When the opening manager of a store in North Carolina opened his store the next day, he wasn't sure who was supposed to do what, and whether some of the changes were implemented or not. To figure out what needed to be done, he had to go through the price point signs to figure out which marketing visual and which pricing went on which specific product.

Since it was Christmas, the store was slammed. The opening manager was caught up focusing on go-backs, helping customers, and trying to find another associate to come in because someone called in sick. He didn't have the time to search through emails to find the proper instructions for the displays.

Other stores struggled as well, confused by what they were responsible for, and what they were expected to do. The busiest shopping time of the year didn't help with the stress, and several stores ended up implementing their own survival strategy. The promotion directions from headquarters never got implemented the way they envisioned, and sales across the board continued to slump.

Unsurprisingly, Fashionistas did not beat their sales record from the previous year.

WHAT'S THE PROBLEM?

Misalignment is a common problem within retail companies. In our example above, a lot went wrong for a single holiday promotion.

The first step to establishing an aligned organization is understanding what it means for a company to be aligned. In retail, everyone's work depends on another's. Every member of the organization plays a role in bringing the brand vision to life. Misalignment happens when people are unclear about their role or responsibility within the company, which can negatively affect sales and customer experience—among other things.

We liken a retail team to a crew on a boat. Every person on that boat needs to know what their role is in moving the boat forward. If everyone is pulling in a different direction, that's not alignment, and instead, they're pulling the organization apart.

If an individual store is not selling well, their shortcomings are usually caused by a lack of alignment from above. The success of a store depends on every department—from the executive suite down to storage. If all of these areas have competing priorities and communicate different instructions to stores, this predictably creates confusion. It's important to define the critical few for the organization to strive for versus the important many.

Misunderstandings can, and do, happen, meaning there is often a disconnect between initial leadership decisions and the way these are shared with the rest of the company. Changes are often ineffectively communicated, meaning people are unclear about which initiatives to be working on. One employee could hear a promotion has been changed from 30 percent to 50 percent off, while another hears the new figure is 40 percent off. People then waste time trying to figure out who was right, discussing who they received communication from, what time the update was received, and what level of the organization it came from. We saw this happen at Fashionistas early on when the communications executive had different information than the marketing director.

STEPS TO CREATING ALIGNMENT

Context Matters

Individual stores are notified about business decisions. What they miss, however, is the context in which that decision was made and the strategy behind it. If leadership labels a store as high line or low line, for example, it is helpful for that store to understand why they fall under that category. This information should also be well known among all the employees within each store.

Misalignment often happens due to a lack of context. If a store doesn't understand the strategy behind production, why they are being identified a certain way, or how they fit into specific groups, they might self-identify incorrectly, like we saw in our Fashionistas example.

The Fashionistas stores didn't understand what the strategy was, specifically regarding the change in promotion after the weekend. So, they spent a lot more on labor because they didn't understand that the strategy was actually to highlight key category products for the Christmas promotion to drive sell-through. The visual wasn't cohesive because they didn't have the whole picture to understand the strategy. They also misplaced some of the marketing signs because the price point seemed similar to some other products. It was a mess.

Since the execution wasn't consistent between the stores, the brand image was ruined. The stores didn't know how to manage the customer confusion, and headquarters didn't understand why execution wasn't happening.

People want to know the "why" behind decisions. It gives them clarity and offers them a sense of ownership. Imagine a clothing retailer with stores in various locations. One is a city store, and another is part of a strip mall. Although they belong to the same retailer, these stores likely have different merchandising or visual display standards. Let's say headquarters instructed the city store to feature black and gray sweaters in their visual displays because they will resonate with urban customers. If headquarters fails to explain the reason behind this decision, that store manager might decide instead their customers will respond more positively to pink floral visual displays. He is wrong, and it causes sales to decrease. They were misaligned to corporate's expectation as to what should be delivered in-store because corporate failed to offer context for why they wanted the store to use black and gray sweaters.

Corporate headquarters likely has more data on why each store fits into a specific category, and how each should be run based on that classification. More important than owning this data, however, is being able to effectively communicate it to the individual store managers. Store managers bring instructions to life. They are in charge of executing tasks, and the way they decide to approach this execution affects how the business will advance. Eliminate confusion and make sure each store manager knows what they are doing and why. Set a standard for execution that managers, and their employees, can strive for.

The Customer Experience

When a customer walks into a store, they expect to be positively received by friendly and knowledgeable staff members. If a store fails to meet that expectation, the customer is left confused and might be discouraged from coming back. Nobody likes messy displays or products placed in the wrong location either. Once you know your customer expectations, you can do everything in your power to meet and exceed those.

To be successful, we all know that a retail store needs to provide a high-quality customer experience. The better the alignment within a company, the more satisfied the customer will be. Every brand has (or at least should have!) an idea of how they want to present themselves. If a customer visits the same store in two states and finds them to be drastically different, the customer is being misled about the brand as a whole.

Don't be like fast food. You've probably walked into McDonald's and had different experiences. Retail shouldn't be like that. Retail customers notice—and appreciate—consistency.

Although it is much easier to effect change online, the value of change is greater in stores. Many retailers spend on the digital because of the reward and tractability. Online, however, retailers don't have complete control over customer experience. A well-designed website will never replace friendly, knowledgeable staff members.

The store is not just the place to make a transaction. It is the focal point for marketing and interacting with customers. The average customer spending triples in-store compared to online. If a customer spends an average of fifty dollars online, their average in-store transaction will be $150. While the digital world is definitely important, business owners should focus on motivating their in-store employees to provide the best experience for their customers. When there is alignment and employees understand their role, executives can introduce changes and employees will feel comfortable making those changes. Not only do they feel comfortable on an individual level, but they understand how these executive decisions help drive the overall business forward.

Visibility

It is important to provide visibility for everyone in the company. Just like stores need to understand business decisions, executives need to be informed about how these decisions are playing out in each individual store. CEOs are not as distanced from their stores as some might think. The CEO of Nike, for example, walks into stores to confirm whether the changes they have implemented have been carried out.

When faced with decreasing sales, for example, a CEO could decide to invest marketing dollars in a specific on-trend product. Hours are spent remerchandising and planning a product launch. Their involvement doesn't end with them giving instructions to their employees, however. If a CEO were to walk into one of their stores, they would need to see their vision made into a reality. All too often CEOs are surprised, though. They don't understand why, if they gave an instruction to put up thirty green-colored marketing signs, this was not carried out. This is a sign of a misaligned organization in which directions sent from the top either fail to go down to stores or are somehow misinterpreted along the way.

In an aligned organization, the executive team doesn't just make decisions and delegate responsibilities, they also keep track of how their instructions are being carried out according to the overall brand vision.

Retailers often test potential new products in certain stores. To obtain accurate and useful data from these experiments, the tests need to be properly aligned. If headquarters decide to test a pair of jeans, for example, every level of the company needs to be aware of the test and understand their role in making it happen. The company headquarters are in charge of communicating the details of the test to each store. If only specific stores have been chosen for experimentation, the district managers need to know which stores to instruct and which to not. The stores themselves should know if they are a test store to prioritize the test above other tasks. If every step in the experimentation process is aligned, a company will receive consistent data and will have effectively tested the product. If not, the test is nothing but a waste of time and money, as the data will be false and corrupted.

Eliminate Internal Competition

For the retail boat to move forward, the different departments need to focus on the same goal. Misalignment happens when an individual store receives conflicting communication from various departments, which creates competing priorities. When the HR, finance, and marketing departments are all sending instructions, how can a store differentiate the critical messages from the less important ones?

We worked with a high-end company in which the executives had a specific vision as to what they wanted the stores to execute and how. When those executives walked out of the boardroom, they were under the impression that the stores would make their vision a reality. The problem was that they had no visibility into whether their instructions were being properly carried out. What frequently happens in a misaligned organization is that executive ideas are filtered through multiple departments before getting to the stores. Along the way, the finance department could introduce an update that dilutes the original executive message.

Simultaneously to the executives trying to move the business, all of the other departments were competing for the store's time and attention. Departments, districts, or territories sent communication directly to stores, meaning the executives had no control over this information or how stores would interpret it alongside headquarters' instructions. This was an organizational flaw. With all the confusion, stores couldn't prioritize their tasks properly, meaning some of the most important tasks failed to get done. A leadership team cannot drive their organization in a coherent direction if every department clutters the roadway with tasks and instructions they consider important.

We like to think of it as a jigsaw puzzle. If every person knows which pieces they are supposed to work on, the puzzle will come together. Say a store is preparing for a holiday. The marketing employees take responsibility for the visuals. The district managers know to inspect stores. The regional directors are responsible for building relationships with community leaders, and the territory leaders are analyzing sales to create growth strategies.

Each department, whether it be marketing, inventory, finance, or operations, is working together to effectively distribute its inventory between stores. Not only are the lines of division clear, but they are properly aligned with each other. If there needs to be a sudden change during the holiday, all employees can immediately identify that change. In a misaligned company, there is often too much chaos for people to recognize a change in business strategy and execute it well.

Set Expectations

The key to an aligned organization is for every person to under-stand their role. And what is the key to every person under-standing their role? Communication. It's the executive team's responsibility to streamline the way they communicate infor-mation and target it to the appropriate audiences.

We once carried out an exercise with retail employees, chal-lenging them to look at the last eighty messages from their executives and highlight each according to its urgency and pri-ority. The messages contained either critical, important, or normal information. The employees' opinions about the critical messages were divided. If the employees of a company cannot identify high-priority information, it is unlikely that they will be able to carry out the tasks expected of them. Internal alignment is critical for employees to understand which instructions are most important and why. The executive team needs to set expec-tations about how to identify urgent information so employees can prioritize the work that needs to get done.

Create Alignment

Nobody likes to waste time. People spend their time more wisely when an organization is better aligned. Employees know their priorities for each day, week, and month. They know they're doing their job and not someone else's. When everybody properly understands their role, more time is spent on jobs that matter. If marketing knows the exact discount figure and implements accurate signs in stores, they can focus their efforts on more strategic jobs like driving traffic. This is a much more effective use of an employee's time than redoing hundreds of price point signs. Imagine a marketing employee is in charge of putting up sixty different price point signs and a figure was miscommunicated, misinterpreted, or changed. That employee would have to redo all sixty signs. An aligned organization both frees up and redirects people's time toward more valuable tasks.

The more visibility district managers have, the better they understand headquarters' objectives and strategies. There is no time wasted on making sense of communication. They don't walk into stores and focus on more minor matters, like whether their fire extinguisher is in the right place, or if they've completed the paperwork for employee benefits. Instead, they can focus on the high-touch, high-value activities like coaching, leadership training, and hiring quality talent. These activities are much harder to teach people through email or over the phone, and require a motivated, focused, and dedicated manager.

Retailers often rely on federal planning because the levels of a company lack visibility into what the other levels are doing. They can't plan out the growth rate of an individual employee or store, for example. They aren't sure what it means to assign a manageable workload. More aligned organizations have a more resourceful approach to work. They can assign work in digestible ways because the organization as a whole is aligned with people's priorities for each day, week, and month. Without visibility, instructions are being sent left, right, and center. These instructions are either conflicting or repetitive and distract from the overall flow of the business.

There is better accountability when one has a clear under-standing of their responsibilities. Accountability is important in retail, because workforces are often seasonal and the general manager will not always be in-store.

If there is ambiguity about a person's role, someone didn't communicate effectively. The upper field of a company—the vice presidents, regional managers, and district managers—should focus on people rather than tactics. They are in charge of dele-gating responsibility to the rest of the employees. This needs to be clearly communicated so each person can be held accountable for the role they have been assigned.

The distributive nature of retail management requires a higher level of alignment than is necessary in headquarters. Retail businesses have stores in different states or locations around the world. In headquarters, it's much easier to direct a change. All it takes is to stop by someone's desk or call for a staff meeting. District managers, however, cannot always stop by and keep every one of their stores on track.

An aligned and dynamic organization has better planning and accountability as well as a more efficient cascade of work. With less confusion, the speed of the business increases. In an effectively aligned company, like Banana Republic or TOMS, for example, there is a high level of visibility. Executives communicate with each other. They talk about what they are asking stores to do and when. This way, they can also avoid conflict when scheduling changes. With a high level of visibility, executives can create bet-ter strategies about running the business, and then follow how these strategies play out in the different levels of the company.

WHERE TO START

A retail business with a misaligned organization is destined for failure. People need to understand their responsibilities in order to do them effectively. Every employee is one piece in the puzzle of a company. For the pieces to come together, people need to understand their roles and have their tasks communicated to them clearly and efficiently. The context of business decisions should be made clear too. Visibility can eliminate competing priorities, emphasizing the common vision of the company.

Ask yourself the following questions to understand your next steps:

1. What are the critical few versus the important many (and what's the priority level)?

2. What happens when it's more important to one department than another? What are the resolution steps?

3. What are the guidelines that we can all internally agree to?

4. Who needs to know what information?

5. What's the best way to deliver that information?

6. What expectations should be set for each person, and should everyone know the expectations of others?

7. How do we create cadence and time the information to support the work?

Remember, you want your boat to move forward. It's vital to make sure every member of your company knows their role in doing so.

Once a company is aligned, the next step is to create clear, intent-based communication channels to help set expectations about what people should be doing and when, which we will cover in the next chapter. The clearer this communication and the more visibility among the channels, the more aligned people will be to what is expected of them.

KEY TAKEAWAYS

- Give stores context about how they fit into the overall brand and why their work matters.

- Maximize visibility about the communication that goes into stores and how initiatives come to life alongside other initiatives.

- Set expectations about the different levels of importance within communication. If messages are urgent and high priority, make that clear.

- Target expectations and communications to make sure the right audiences are receiving the right information at the right time.

- Ensure everyone knows what they should be working on and the business is moving in a unified direction.

Chapter 3

PRINCIPLE 2:
ESTABLISH INTENT-BASED COMMUNICATION CHANNELS

AS WE PREVIOUSLY MENTIONED in the introduction, many retailers think they *don't* have a communication problem—and we totally understand why.

It's not that retailers fail at communication—we've seen plenty of beautifully designed newsletters, perfectly timed emails, engaging chat rooms, and tightly organized tasks. What we don't see, however, is lining up each communication channel with a specific intention.

Many retailers rely on more than one communication tool to spread information through their company. Different communication channels satisfy different objectives, and when done properly, they're incredibly effective. Unfortunately, most retailers don't think in these terms, and their communication channels end up not doing the job they were intended to do.

PROBLEMATIC COMMUNICATION PRACTICES

A lot of our clients tend to use several communication tools, but we've noticed that they tend to heavily rely on one more than others. Here are a few examples of problematic communication practices and outcomes (perhaps you can relate to some of them!).

Email Overload

One of our clients, let's call them Lenzmo, called us to help with their communication strategy. Lenzmo has about one hundred stores across the United States. The communications manager told us his stores were super overwhelmed, so we asked him to conduct an audit of what communications each store was receiving throughout the year to see if we could see why.

He found that over the course of one year, 3,500 messages were sent through email. These emails included information ranging from visual display setups, to employee contests through technology rollouts, to inventory ordering information. On top of that, he was also sending reminder emails. He basically doubled his message count because he didn't trust that his stores would remember the information he sent two weeks ago.

We asked him if his stores received any emails from other

people or departments. He took a look at the cumulative emails for a single store and found that they were also receiving emails from their district manager, their regional director, and their visual specialist—in addition to even more emails between the store leadership themselves. On top of that, some stores were also receiving emails from community partners that they formed partnerships with to help drive traffic to both stores.

So, the 3,500 emails from our first chat were *from just him.*

When we talked to some of the stores, they were struggling and (not surprisingly) confused. They often didn't know whether the email was meant for every store, or whether it was a select store message that the communications manager was sending separately. Stores also often found conflicting messages in the updates that were sent later.

To make matters worse, their district managers were sending different updates than what the stores were receiving from headquarters—no one was on the same page. The stores were getting crushed under this mountain of emails that was impossible to manage. Email works when the goal is to inform and delegate, but it's not a great tool to keep track of whether the tasks were completed; there's no way of knowing that through this communication channel.

This dependency on email at Lenzmo caused major inefficiency in terms of information, quality, and volume. Stores weren't spending the time on the right things because they spent most of their time trying to piece together the instructions from these emails. They were simply trying to figure out what they needed to do.

With email overload, some people simply checked out and stopped reading the emails altogether.

Chat Fatigue

A small boutique, let's call them Roma's Boutique, wanted to communicate in a more dynamic way, especially since they only had thirty stores. They had a SharePoint site, but because they were a high-touch business where they wanted to coach and train their employees, they also wanted to have more fluid conversations between teams, headquarters, and stores. Roma's Boutique therefore decided to set up Yammer, one of several free chat sites available (like Salesforce, Chatter, Workplace by Facebook, etc.) and use that as their primary communications channel.

The visual team jumped right in and initiated chats with stores. They started using the chat site to send visual merchandising directions and planograms. They used the platform to also answer any questions the stores had. In the beginning, everyone thought it was awesome because people were engaged. It's so easy to communicate! Stores weren't confused about directions, mannequins were wearing the correct products and positioned in the right locations, and customers responded well to the thoughtful presentations. It worked so well, in fact, that other departments, like marketing and merchandising, also set up their own group chats and started sending out information to the stores.

Visual then started to add more stores to the conversation, and as more and more stores joined the chat, the volume of discussions and threads soon became overwhelming. Stores were forced to scroll through endless threads—often useless and saturated with various opinions and commentary from different stores. After spending extra time catching up reading through the threads, several stores grew confused with the information overload. Not only was visual adding more stores, so were the other departments. Now stores had to go through several chat groups to figure out what the directions and expectations were. During one month, merchandising sent out a product test to a select group of stores, but they posted about it in the merchandising channel for all the stores to see. Several stores panicked, thinking they missed important instructions, when in reality, they weren't a part of the selected stores to test out the product in the first place.

Because there was so much chatter in between all the different channels, people could not keep track of the work. There was no way to bookmark or star any directions either. The search feature was not functional, so stores couldn't find the message string that they wanted. As a result, stores grew frustrated. More and more people were piling into the system looking for direction and sending contradictory information.

This also led to a lack of accountability because people felt like if they just put something out there, then their job was done, versus checking to see if, first, the communication reached the right person and, second, if it was executed.

The One-Stop Shop That No One Visits

Another client of ours, we'll call them Lorallie's, tried a one-stop-shop approach and posted all of their communication on a

SharePoint site. This was meant to be a go-to site where employees could find daily messages, to-dos, expectations, directions on promotions, and so on—basically everything. When things changed, an email announcing the change was sent, instructing stores to go reference the site.

The advantage with this setup is that everyone knows where to go to get the latest information. Theoretically, stores would have access to the latest version of the truth.

When we dug in, however, the reality was that no one was using SharePoint because it was difficult to access. The search function was poor, so people couldn't find what they needed quickly and efficiently. To make things worse, due to the fear of losing the post, people started downloading attachments and printing them out to put on their desks. Some regional managers, knowing the site was hard to use, downloaded the attachments and forwarded them to their stores through email. If an update or change was issued, then another document would be forwarded, but now Lorallie's had two versions of an attachment about the same thing out there—one wrong, one right. Were people looking at the right one?

Another functionality SharePoint doesn't offer is the follow through: did everyone see the post? There's no way of knowing whether the stores saw the communication or not. Lorallie's headquarters sent an email to all of its stores with news that the product promotion for Labor Day weekend was raised to 50 percent off instead of 20 percent, and then instructed the stores to check SharePoint. But because district managers didn't know whether the stores saw the information or not, they texted, called, or emailed their stores to confirm that they did. This extra communication shouldn't be necessary, as it only adds more work.

Another problem with portals is their lack of functionality on mobile devices. Oftentimes, people receive their email on their phone just fine, but in order to follow a link to read a PDF, for example, they have to go through a VPN on their phone, and then a bunch of authentication. Well, that's a hassle, so they end up not doing it. One regional manager for Lorallie's, because he was traveling, waited until he was near a desktop computer to open and read the PDF. By then, the information was already outdated and the regional manager—and his stores—missed out on implementing the proper instructions.

WHAT'S THE PROBLEM?

All three examples illustrate the various things that could go wrong when using one primary communication channel. Because the retailers focused on sending all communications through one avenue, employees became confused, overwhelmed, and withdrawn. Their work ended up being doubled, as they wasted time looking for information. The same information is often communicated in different ways, which is a waste of time and effort; or two separate communications can give contradictory instructions.

An executive could send out a well-designed and informative newsletter about an event, but this is rendered useless because it gets lost in an overload of emails about event updates. A district manager might instruct a store one thing, while an email from headquarters says another, as we saw with the Lenzmo example. As a result, stores don't know which instructions to follow.

While each communication method has value, there isn't a holy grail, one-stop-shop option. Retailers need to establish intent-based communication channels that relay specific communication types.

WHAT'S THE SOLUTION?

Different types of information need to be communicated throughout the year, and not all information is created equal. A chat from a coworker doesn't have the same priority as an email from the SVP of a company. However, all of these communications can, and should, exist together to provide context for everyone.

To properly communicate information, it is necessary to classify it into categories. Once you do that, you can choose the communication vehicle that best supports the information in each category.

We've found that there are four distinct types of communication that happen in retail:

- "Nice-to-know" information

- "Need-to-know" information

- "Evergreen content"

- "Dialogue, discussion, and debate"

Nice-to-Know

"Nice-to-know" information makes people feel good. It's not directly actionable but is important because it builds brand camaraderie and morale. It could include a letter from the president of a company, congratulatory messages, social media posts, new partnerships, or community events. This information is beneficial and helps build employee morale, which is important in keeping everyone engaged. Nice-to-know information is worth communicating, but it isn't groundbreaking or exactly mandatory for employees to read. Portals, like SharePoint, support this sort of information best.

Need-to-Know

"Need-to-know" information is actionable and time based. This includes tasks that need to be completed, or the basic expectations of the business, which could include implementing new signs, fixing fitting room signs, changing pamphlets, or creating terms and conditions for a marketing event. This information is mandatory. Need-to-know information is often associated with a date, like a sale event. An inventory count falls under need-to-know information, for example. It is actionable, and involves employees counting out the styles and products they have in-store and comparing these to the overall stock available. There is a problem if a customer orders a product that a store claims to have but actually doesn't. An inventory count can resolve this problem, but stores need to know when this should be completed.

Task managers, like Teamwork, are the most effective for transmitting need-to-know information, especially since they offer a way of communicating that the tasks have been completed.

Evergreen Content

"Evergreen content" is long-term, live-long information. The information is important, but not always immediately actionable. It should be stored in a company library and referenced when necessary. This could include resource guides, employee handbooks, seasonal training standards, successful business practices, healthcare benefits, and instructions for ordering supplies and submitting payrolls, among others. Every company and store has this information, although it might not automatically be on hand. It doesn't change day over day or week over week as much. It's more fixed.

File managers, like Box, best support evergreen content. Having this information stored on a portal works well because it's fixed content that is easy to get to and is referenceable. Live-long content should have a fixed URL (meaning it doesn't change) so that it can be bookmarked.

Dialogue, Discussion, and Debate

The last type of communication, "dialogue, discussion, and debate," is an opportunity for the people in your company to share ideas and brainstorm. This form of communication is more casual and conversational. It is chat based and encourages employees to contribute their own suggestions to benefit the company. Perhaps a manager wants to drive a pet fair in front of their store to increase traffic. The manager and his team could start a discussion and bounce their ideas off of one another. Maybe another manager has carried out a similar fair and can offer some ideas about how best to execute the idea.

Slack and Yammer are effective for this type of communication.

WHAT DOES SUCCESSFUL INTENT-BASED COMMUNICATION LOOK LIKE?

Many retailers compile these four types of communication into emails or portal sites, but this causes confusion about where people should look for what they need. Many retailers use chat channels to share all of the information in one go. We do not recommend this because expectations are unclear.

Although the channels themselves might be effective, the nice-to-know information is not of the same priority as the need-to-know information. Retailers can communicate much more successfully if they create distinct channels for different purposes and make clear what those purposes are.

For example, say a retailer introduces a new product line inspired by a celebrity. Nice-to-know information for the line could include engaging videos with designers talking about the look and their inspiration, or pictures of the merchant's travels to source the product. This type of content is worthy of sharing and could be uploaded on the portal page of the company's website. Social media can help to engage employees and get them excited about upcoming products.

However, there is also information that people *need* to know about the line. The date that the product comes into stores is important to clarify, as is the amount of product coming in. Stores need to know how the visual displays should be arranged. They should have a firm understanding of what the lighting should look like, how the outfit should be styled on the mannequin, and which posters should go in the windows. If the celebrity is going to make an appearance, this should be announced well in advance for everyone to prepare. Many retailers rely on task management tools for this type of communication.

The evergreen content for this line could include the best practices for merchandising, the product colors, how shipping is processed, how the brand typically merchandises their products, how clothes are standardized from left to right on the hanger, or the way lighting is set up according to red, green, and yellow hues. This content constitutes a foundational layer and sets the standard for operating across stores. These are the live-long resources that stores can pull from their libraries and file managers.

The dialogue, discussion, and debate drives and increases excitement about the product. People could discuss the best practices for upselling, ideas about extensions, and customer feedback. One employee could have kids who are excited about the celebrity partnership, for example. They could use this channel to discuss whether any marketing is specifically targeting children.

Someone else could be curious about any other products that sell successfully alongside the new product line.

All four types of communication are important, but they should be distinguished so the information is properly interpreted.

STEPS TO CREATING SUCCESSFUL INTENT-BASED COMMUNICATION CHANNELS

Establish Structure

It's imperative for companies to establish structure for these four types of communication so they don't have chaos and leakage with information being inaccessible. As a retailer, it's your responsibility to identify the pros and cons of each communication method and decide which works best for each purpose. We recommend portals for nice-to-know information, task managers for need-to-know information, file managers for evergreen content, and chats like Chatter or Yammer for dialogue, discussion, and debate. These are our suggestions, however, and we encourage you to figure out what makes the most sense for you and your company.

After identifying the different types of communication, we recommend building a framework that supports all four categories from a technological and content perspective. In a practical sense, this means piecing together a file manager system, chat system, or task manager to create a one-stop-shop communication channel to fit your company.

A retailer is also responsible for creating expectations for their team about how each type of communication should be used, what it's for, and where to find it. Not only should people recognize the purpose of nice-to-know information, but they should know to look in your portal to find it. If an employee wants to share an idea for a potential sale, they should know to jump on Yammer to do so, not through the portal or through email. Without establishing clear destinations for information, your team will struggle to understand where to go for what.

Listen to Feedback

Once you launch a communication framework, listen to the feedback from your team. If they don't like a communication method or find it difficult to use, that likely means they are not getting the relevant information (because they will simply stop using it!). The last thing you want is for your team to avoid using your channels because they aren't user friendly. Listen to their feedback to update the communication tools you've chosen and see if there is something that better suits you and your team.

Fine-Tune

The good news is that almost every retailer we've met already has the necessary communication tools in place. They use email and likely have files on a network drive. Retailers need to take the next step, however, and fine-tune their communication types and find the appropriate channels for each (and then educate their team on each channel's intention).

Look to your communication team to function as the central communication for your company. They should be responsible for connecting the work for people in a clear and easy-to-understand format. The communication team may not be the business owner, but they function as a conduit for your brand's voice—which should permeate from the inside out. They deliver the information necessary for the brand to function. No matter how important the information, it is useless if ineffectively communicated.

BENEFITS TO IMPLEMENTING DIFFERENT TYPES OF COMMUNICATION

Intent-based communication goes hand in hand with aligned organization, and that's why it's our second principle. With alignment, the different departments of an organization know their role and are working in a unified direction. In an aligned organization, communication will naturally become more streamlined. Once a person is clear about their individual role, they need access to the relevant information to carry out that role, which is where the communication comes in.

Implementing different types of communication offers many benefits. It will help control the noise that often comes out of the various things retailers have to communicate throughout the year. When everything is in real time, the noise increases (which often leads to confusion, disengagement, and chaos among employees). Controlling the noise means less time is spent searching through emails or threads, trying to find the appropriate tasks for each store.

Speaking of a better use of everyone's time, intent-based communication creates an automatic filter for employees of how to best use their time. They'll know to make sure to read need-to-know information right away, and if they don't have time to brainstorm ideas in Yammer because they're working on executing a task, they can forgo checking the chat without worrying that they're missing something important. People work differently, and thus should have the option to communicate as much or as little as they want. You're giving people a choice in how much they want to engage with the brand. Some people will be brand cheerleaders, while others are just there to execute what is expected of them and then go home.

The clarity established with intent-based communication means you can effectively drive your business forward. You'll no longer have to worry whether a store received direction from above, or whether they executed it. You'll no longer have to worry about employees wasting their time reading through thousands of emails or long chat threads, looking for relevant information. Employees will know exactly where to go to get the necessary things done, so your brand can thrive.

Now that you understand the benefits of establishing different types of communication, you might be wondering about what and when to send such information, which we'll cover in the next chapter.

KEY TAKEAWAYS

- There are four categories of information in retail: nice-to-know information, need-to-know information, evergreen content, and dialogue, discussion, and debate.

- Recognize the difference between the four categories and identify which communication channels work best for each type of information.

- Set up distinct channels and create expectations so people know what the information is for and how it should be used.

- Create clear destinations so people know where each type of information can be found.

- Adjust your communication framework based on the feedback from your team.

Chapter 4

PRINCIPLE 3:
SEND THE RIGHT MESSAGE
AT THE RIGHT TIME

WE LIVE IN A DYNAMIC DIGITAL AGE, and the retail-store experience has changed significantly over the years. Customer shopping patterns today are much different than they were twenty years ago. Customers now enjoy making purchases online and then picking their items up in-store, for example. Some retailers even offer lockers where people can pick up their mailing packages.

The ways retailers operate, however, have not changed. There is a huge disconnect between retailers and meeting their customer's expectations because they're still using old models of deaf practices, like operations and communication.

The pace of business is also changing—and it seems to grow faster and faster by the day! While many businesses snail mail information to their stores up to six months in advance, that's just not practical anymore.

Target, for example, had an amazing planning process. Everything was extremely structured and well-oiled. They planned about a year out, and then broke that year out into certain milestones (one at eight months and then another at six months out, for example). They'd create packets and send them out to all their stores. Stores had time to sort through all the material (calendars, event details, planograms, etc.), and plan according to what was coming up. Lots of retailers still employ this strategy, but because customer shopping patterns have changed significantly (and because people are a lot more reactive to business), we just don't have that lead time anymore. We don't have the luxury to plan so far in advance since the landscape is changing too fast.

So what did retailers like Target do? They evolved. Instead of sending huge, beautifully put together packets via physical mail, they adapted it to email. And instead of planning a year out, they would plan in smaller chunks, and send the appropriate instructions on an ongoing basis.

CURRENT COMMUNICATION CHALLENGES

Moving to email was clearly a step in the right direction, but as business, technology, and our customer expectations continue to change rapidly, the communication most retailers currently employ is not keeping up. The following are the most common messaging practices.

Ongoing Messaging

Many retailers create cadences of communication to manage the volume of information they need to transmit. These typically include communication bundles that are sent in quarterly, monthly, biweekly, or even weekly cadences.

Although the intention of moving the information from mailed-out packets into email was the right move, the execution exposed certain unique challenges. Although the plan was to send information periodically, that was rarely the case. The biggest problem with weekly communication is that it is never actually weekly—it somehow always turns into daily!

Oftentimes, stores receive twenty to eighty communications a week. Headquarters will, for example, send PDF packets of information to stores with different themes every Monday. The stores then try to piece together what they should do, according to their store category. Maybe one particular Monday is unusually busy, or perhaps someone called in sick, and tasks from the PDF weren't completed. "No worries," the manager might say. "We'll finish it first thing tomorrow morning." But then the next morning, another piece of communication comes in that conflicts with what was sent on Monday. The store now needs to figure out if what they did needs to change based on the new details, and the manager is spending more time just trying to figure out what his store still needs to do.

Being able to process and digest all of the information just isn't realistic.

One of our clients, Berme (not their real name), implemented a weekly communication cadence, but also sent out a daily update.

Berme made it clear that the daily communication superseded the weekly, which then caused the stores to spend a lot of time flipping back and forth between what they read in the weekly communication and what changed in the daily update. Another client also decided to go with a weekly cadence, but then they set expectations for their stores to also check their email twice a day—once at 10 a.m. and the second at 5 p.m.—to make sure nothing was sent out from headquarters. What's the point of establishing a weekly communication when they're asking their stores to check their email twice a day?

These companies have structures in place, but in reality, there are so many messages leaking out—critical ones, no less—that it's defeating the purpose of a planned communication. One way retailers have tried to deal with the leakage is by implementing *themed communication* three times a week. For example, communication relating to loss prevention and human resources will be sent out on Monday; marketing and promotions on Wednesday; and inventory and merchandising on Friday. Their hope was to give stores a more digestible way to go through and understand what's expected of them and what actions they need to take to materially drive the business. Unfortunately, it doesn't work because—again—business happens twenty-four hours a day, and it's constantly changing. It's not like when you read the news, you only read natural disasters on one day and politics the next day. Timely communication should change to reflect the dynamics of what's happening within that organization.

On the flip side, other retailers commit to the weekly cadence and will wait until the next scheduled communication to announce any changes or updates. This isn't advisable either. With how fast things move in retail these days, your store will miss out and business will inevitably go down. In our pitch to send the right message at the right time, these retailers miss the mark altogether.

The point of ongoing messaging is because business is running twenty-four hours a day. We need to set good routines and behaviors for people to follow, but we also need to deliver information to them in real time because business changes. We need to deliver communication in more digestible and bite-sized ways, so stores aren't spending a half an hour reading our messages. It's about establishing a consistent stream of digestible information. Think of a fire hose; instead of drinking out of a blasting stream of water, how do you reduce the flow so that it's more of a constant stream that is more predictable—not to mention more enjoyable to drink out of.

Seasonal Messaging

When it comes to seasonal messages—whether that's Christmas, Back to School, or Fourth of July—sending them at the right time is imperative due to the natural timeliness of these communications. Most retailers take seasonal planning to mean taking more time to plan, which is what they typically do. With seasonal messaging, it is common for retailers to revert to the old school method.

To make things more complicated, big retailers often invite other departments to help with the seasonal planning. In our experience, 70 to 80 percent of retailers implement cross-functional planning processes for these peak seasons. Take Hommel, for example (yep, we changed its name).

Hommel invited a group of people from marketing, merchandising, inventory, design, and operations to put together their holiday communications plan for the year. Three to five months before October, this team of people from different departments gathered content, came up with taglines, and put together a fairly large seasonal binder with different tabs (a planning tab, a sales tab, a visual tab, and so on). Hommel's team did an excellent job designing the binder, too; it was beautiful.

Once approved, the files are off to the printer, and then they're sent to the stores. The stores were instructed to use the binders throughout the entire season, and all the instructions and plans were right there at their fingertips. At first, Hommel's stores felt great because they felt prepared. They all received a one-hundred-page binder of everything they needed to know for the entire season. But once the season finally arrived, things quickly changed. People and sales changed over. The stores might have been prepared for the basic, live-long retail practices, but they were missing the timelier and more specific information for those holidays. After a few weeks, Hommel's average transaction size was down, so headquarters decided to add a contest. Certain pieces of product weren't selling as well as they should have, so they also changed the outfitting strategy.

Well, neither of those changes were in the binder.

Because everything was printed in the binder—and it was supposed to be this holistic, seasonal, one-stop shop—they weren't able to update in real time, so it quickly grew outdated. One week into their peak season, and Hommel's seasonal binder (that multiple departments spent months on!) was no longer relevant.

Not only was the seasonal binder a waste of time (how long did it take to put together?) and money (how many people were paid in its creation? How much was printing and shipping?), it ended up also causing confusion at the store level. Although printed binders can be beautifully designed, their functionality for the way retail operates in this day and age is no longer realistic.

Thankfully, Hommel soon changed their practices. They distributed an internal marketing piece about the best general practices, and then throughout the rest of the holiday season, they focused on timelier communication, providing updates and changes daily. This was much more effective preparation for their stores.

Random Messaging

Another type of messaging we see, mostly with smaller retailers, is communication that comes off cadence, or what we like to call *random messaging*.

Rosewood, a small retailer in Colorado with about twenty stores, established a structured communication cadence that worked fairly well. One day, however, the CEO decided to email the stores in the middle of the day with some direction she wanted implemented. She didn't want to wait four days for the next communication cadence to go out. Out of sync with its normal cadence, her email shocked the system for everyone who worked there. "Oh shoot! The CEO emailed us! She needs us to do something. Quick! Stop what you're doing and let's do this thing."

Not only did the email disrupt the day's cadence, it also left some other unintended effects. Now the stores were wary that the CEO could email them at any moment. Store managers grew concerned they might miss something, so they started to constantly check their email more than usual. This ever-looming concern became difficult for people to manage. It put them in a state of uncertainty because they'd been trained to receive a weekly cadence, and then the CEO's random messaging threw them out of...well...cadence.

Any messaging that's not part of a structured process becomes surprising or difficult. The problem is when there is a sudden and urgent piece of information that retailers need to communicate immediately. In retail, this happens all the time. Despite setting specific days for communication, business owners often break their own cadence rules and email their employees outside of those times, like we saw with Rosewood.

Unknown/Unstructured Messaging

If you were to walk into some retail stores and ask about their communication cadence, many employees don't even realize there is one. Unfortunately, some stores have become used to their communication being all over the place. They get information at different times and on different days because that's what they've come to expect (which isn't ideal).

When stores receive too much information too often, people either spend too much time sorting through information, or, as we mentioned in the previous chapter, they're too overwhelmed to read through all the messaging, so they check out altogether and end up missing key tasks. We once had a store manager spend two hours trying to find a sale message because she couldn't remember when it was sent. People struggle to pinpoint when certain messages were communicated, which is even more problematic if the information isn't searchable.

In another instance, we spoke with the director of store operations and communication at a high-end luxury store. She explained that communication was chaotic because stores struggled to keep up with the random timing of the messages. The volume in which these messages were sent out was also difficult to keep track of. We asked how the best store managers were approaching the situation, and she said they printed everything out.

E-V-E-R-Y-T-H-I-N-G.

They even printed out information that wasn't applicable to them. Obviously, this is a waste of time that could be spent more productively.

There are many consequences to sending the wrong messages at the wrong times. It creates communication chaos. People are wasting time trying to figure out what they're supposed to do. Stores don't know what to expect, and therefore don't know what is expected of them. The volume of information is too high for people to properly interpret, and as such, tasks fall through the cracks. The brand voice is not consistent from store to store.

Untimely communication is a vicious cycle. People become resigned to the same inefficient habits, leading to poor execution of tasks.

WHAT'S THE SOLUTION?

If a business wants to keep up with such a fast-paced society and stay ahead of its competition, it needs to focus on sending the right message at the right time.

If information is sent too early, it could get lost and forgotten about among other priorities. If the information is sent too late, like the day before, for example, people aren't given enough time to plan and prepare. We need to find a balance between releasing information when it's available and communicating what will be usable to that person at that time. It doesn't make sense to force all the information into the same batch of communication.

Not only should information be communicated in real time, but it should be sent in digestible pieces. Snackable content is more digestible and actionable than gorging on a ton of information all at once. Think of that fire hose. You want to have a steady stream so everyone's in step, moving the business in the right direction. Instead of weekly sporadic movement, how do we move the ship day by day instead of taking these leapfrog movements? When retailers send binders to stores, it's unlikely that all the included information will be absorbed. Equally, stores will feel overwhelmed if they receive three paragraphs of details about an event the day prior. Break down communication. Give people exactly what they need to know when they need to know it. Focus on communicating the information that will support the work people are doing at that time, not months in advance.

Retail is an especially chaotic industry. It is up to the retailers to manage that chaos by establishing a structure that'll set expectations around communication. Think of this framework as a fishing net. Fishing nets are strong, but they are also flexible. A weekly cadence won't allow companies to effectively respond to a sudden competitive sale that threatens their business. The chaotic nature of the retail industry makes it especially important to establish a strong framework for fluid communication. We believe a daily communication cadence to be the most effective form for transmitting timely information.

When you put a system in place for real-time communication, event notifications can be sent in the general stream without overwhelming people. Retailers can send communications as they are necessary, and stores are in a better position to respond to competitive needs without causing confusion.

Well-timed and targeted messages are crucial in giving companies leverage over their competition. Say a manager is closing one of their stores and sees a competitor place a sign for a 20 percent sale on the same pair of jeans that he's also selling. If he had a real- time system in place, he could respond with a competitive sale overnight. The manager could notify headquarters and design a stream of information to be sent to stores first thing the next morning. All the store managers would come in and immediately know what to act on to respond to the competitor's sale.

Real-time communication has strategic benefits if a company has the necessary structures put in place for stores to react effectively. If employees are only expecting to receive sale information every three weeks, they would be caught off guard with such sudden communication and fail to respond to the competition. The goal is for retailers to change that expectation.

The ideal daily cadence will have all the information ready when the store opens. Retailers should teach their employees good habits. If a company has their communication set for midnight, for example, the employees will walk into the store in the morning, make sure they are on top of their daily tasks and general business information, and start their work for the day. It should become instinctual, just like brushing your teeth in the morning.

This doesn't mean there isn't room for less frequent cadences for matters like staffing and planning. It still makes sense for a store manager to sit down on a certain day and schedule staff for two weeks in advance. The manager knows which employees will be most suited for upcoming events. If there is a credit card event happening on a certain date and the manager knows Billy is great at getting people to sign up for brand credit cards, Billy needs to know in advance that he has been staffed for this event. The communications that affect employees' future workloads should be sent in advance for people to plan.

WHAT ABOUT TECHNOLOGY?

Daily cadences are designed to contain the need-to-know information, otherwise known as the operational communication. This could include last minute changes like altering marketing signage, taking down beacons because of safety hazards, or implementing new HR policies. The nice-to-know information can be read at people's own leisure, like on the bus or during a break.

Primarily, the need-to-know information is sent via email. However, some companies successfully use task management systems as well.

Technologically, retailers need to develop strains and habits and encourage people to pay attention to notifications. Imagine a system that generates a daily task list for people. If you train your people to work from that task list, you can add information the night before and know it'll get done because your staff will see it on their list first thing in the morning.

We once worked with a major food and beverage distributor in which one of the store managers was great with people, but horrible with execution. He struggled with task management. When the company implemented daily task lists for their people, that store manager quickly became one of the top-executing employees. He still wasn't the best planner, but his team was great at getting things done. This is a clear example of how daily task lists can help drive a business much faster.

The technology in which you invest can save you a lot of time. If a software creates a calendar for your people, you won't need to send a batch of information for them to plan and prepare their own calendars. With a manual calendar, one person needs to block off enough time to sit, go through all the emails, see which events are coming up, and map out what needs to get done over the next two weeks. Imagine, however, that the next day some new information comes through and doesn't get added to the calendar. That person is then working from an inaccurate manual calendar. Implementing the right channels, whether those are task management or chat and discussion channels, can save a company a lot of back and forth, which frees up time for work that actually matters.

STEPS TO SENDING MESSAGES AT THE RIGHT TIME

Implement Principles 1 and 2 First

We realize that many retailers have probably tried to communicate real-time information before and have been unsuccessful in the past. Instead of providing clarity, their messaging only adds to the overall noise. There is a reason we made this the third principle. The first two principles are crucial in establishing a strong foundation for the third.

Before you think about sending the right message at the right time, make sure your organization is properly aligned and has established intent-based communication channels. For example, a big part of aligning an organization is identifying which audiences require which communication. The same message sent to all of a retailer's stores throughout the US, Canada, and Mexico probably shouldn't be sent at the same time. A message that only applies to Canadian stores shouldn't be sent through a general communication channel accessible by everyone, because people have to wade through information that doesn't apply to them to find what they need to know. Without an audience in mind, the whole idea of targeted communication falls apart. Segment your communication channels to make sure that the right message is not only sent at the right time, but to the right people.

Once a business is genuinely ready for the third principle, the retailer needs to reset expectations about the timing for communications. They should break out of the habit of strict or infrequent cadences. The clearer a retailer is about the new timings they have implemented, the better their business partners can do their work.

There is a tendency to want to communicate information as soon as it's known. Often, there will be communication clashes because people in visual, marketing, and finance will want to send their messages at the same time. However, strategic communication will be far more beneficial for business.

Imagine a business partner decides to mark down merchandise in two days. They want to communicate this to stores immediately. When they make the decision, however, it might be 3 p.m. Pacific Time, meaning East Coast stores are beginning to shut down. If these stores are used to seeing a communication of tasks in the morning, it would be beneficial to wait and send the message at a time when the task will actually be seen and carried out. Although the business partner wants to send their message as quickly as possible, this could end up doing them a disservice. Everyone in the company needs to be led to understand that sending vital information at the wrong time might mean fewer people see the message, lessening the chances that the task will actually get carried out.

Retailers need to set up expectations within their businesses. Usually, the communications team handles the internal communications within a company. However, people are used to following orders from their bosses, meaning the executive team plays a big role in sending the right message at the right time. If the VP of a company gives an instruction to send out a notice immediately, someone in marketing needs to send that instruction to the communications team to include in the morning summary.

Executive pressure is an important factor in driving behavior. Executives tend to buy into daily cadences because if a piece of information needs to be sent, they'll be more willing to wait until the next morning than waiting for the next communication bundle, which is typically frustrating and restrictive. Daily cadences make it a lot easier for executives to have conversations about when information should be sent for tasks to effectively be executed in stores.

Once an organization is well-aligned and has established solid, intent-based communication channels, they are better prepared to develop a strategy to send timelier messages to their employees.

Work in Real Time

Changes aren't an occasional occurrence in retail—oh no. They happen all the time. If you want to stand any sort of chance against your competition, your messaging needs to work in real time.

Let's say an email gets sent about a new merchandising campaign for children's toys. Not long after, the retailer learns that the vendor for one of the toy manufacturers is delayed, which means the campaign launch needs to be updated. The retailer could send an update about the change, but this one-line message would likely get lost in an endless stream of information. It would be more effective for the change to be reworked into the original message. There should be a stamp at the top of the notice with a time, date, and announcement of the change to provide people with context.

Say that two weeks later, the line of toys has been launched, but the traffic isn't as high as expected, so the retailer decides to implement a marketing change. Rather than sending out a singular message about updated marketing, the communications team should alter the original message, which will provide the necessary context for people to understand the marketing change.

Giving people the right information at the right time means giving people context about the updates happening within a business. We recommend establishing continuity. Sending five updates will be ineffective and only confuse employees, making it much harder to track what has changed and when. As a retailer, it's your responsibility to create a system that accounts for continual change and effectively communicates updates so that employees can understand instructions and act on them.

To Email or Not to Email?

If there are no updates on a certain day, does it still make sense to send stores an email because that's what they're used to?

On one hand, people like having less email in their inbox, so it doesn't seem logical to send an email if there isn't a necessity to communicate anything. On the other hand, maybe people like to explicitly hear there is no new information so they don't feel like they're missing something.

When we carried out this test with a major denim retailer, the results showed that people *do want* to receive an email, even if it contains no new information. If people don't receive an email, they either assume the system is broken, they have missed something, or the message has gone to their spam folder.

If people receive an email saying there is nothing new to do or read, they can be certain they are on top of everything, which gives them peace of mind to focus on other tasks. When a retailer establishes a drumbeat of communication, it is important to keep this rhythm as constant as possible. In an industry that revolves around rapid-fire emails and sudden updates, the more comfortable and reassured people can feel, the better work they'll do.

We once did a whiteboard session for Columbus Day and sent out seven different updates about the sale within a two-week period—not the best idea. Store managers struggled to follow and react to all of these updates, and they weren't sure which information to depend on. Confusion set in, and they didn't know what was expected of them.

We suggest retailers establish a system where only critical information is communicated at the last minute. If there needs to be a store lockdown due to suspected violence, for example, this is code red and obviously cannot wait until the next morning's bulletin. The majority of high-priority information, however, can be sent and interpreted effectively in daily cadences.

WHAT ARE THE RESULTS?

When a business learns to send the right message at the right time, the company will become more responsive and competitive. Not only will business executives be able to implement change faster, but they will be able to depend on their people to deliver that change.

Once you align the organization and implement effective communication channels, you can put structures in place that will give people peace of mind about the exact work that needs to get done. If people are receiving the right message at the right time, that means they know what is being asked of them.

The more effective the in-store execution, the more positive the employee's experience. A person's quality of life improves if they feel productive at work because they have been given the right tools to be successful. Employees won't need to redo work if they initially receive the proper communication and know what is expected of them. Retail and grocery industries have the highest turnover for seasonal employees. Targeted and timely communication from an employer will improve the hiring, training, and retaining of employees, which will give the business a better competitive advantage.

We often receive inquiries from companies who want to improve the tools they offer to their employees. A business could hire a store manager, for example, who previously worked at a high-end brand where they were given better tools, technology, and resources to do their job. It is important for retailers to check themselves; there is always room for improvement somewhere.

Sending the right message at the right time allows companies to compete more effectively in their industry, provides peace of mind for retail employees, and makes for a better-quality customer experience. A daily cadence of communication provides employees with expectations about where and when to look for the information they need to do their job.

The better the communication between employer and employee, the more productive the latter will feel. Give your team access to the tools they'll need to be the best working versions of themselves. This will allow them to feel like they are making a difference by working in your company. We've all heard this, but it's true: happy employees equal happy customers. If you want your stores to provide quality customer experience, you need to start with the employees who interact with the people who walk into your stores. Empower your team to make them feel like they matter to your company.

There is a direct correlation between empowered employees and success in business, which we'll discuss more in the following chapter.

KEY TAKEAWAYS

- Daily cadences are the most effective way to support real-time, need-to-know information.

- Employees need to receive communication in digestible chunks and with context. Make sure information supports the work people are doing at that time.

- Last minute changes do happen, and retailers should put structures in place to support these updates.

- Make good use of technology, as it can free up a lot of time for more valuable work.

- Deliver a constant drumbeat of information so people have peace of mind about being on top of their work.

- When businesses learn to send the right message at the right time, they provide better customer service, become more responsive, and have better leverage over their competition.

Chapter 5

PRINCIPLE 4:
EMPOWER YOUR WORKFORCE

RETAIL IS ONE OF THE MOST POPULOUS jobs in America. Because there are so many people and such a high turnover, all too often retail companies fail to empower their employees and give them the relevant context to aid the work they're doing. Every member of a company fits into a brand strategy. To do their work effectively, employees have to see *why* their work matters. They need to feel like they are important to the brand as a whole.

Unfortunately, there are also poor ways of empowering your workforce. We'd like to share a few of them.

Cognitive Dissonance

Some retailers give their stores too much freedom when it comes to interpreting key priorities. A retailer might say, "This clearance event is extremely important to us. It's going to drive business." The retailer will then give stores the high-level view and the why, but not the how.

And that's when we hear about the operational horror stories where duct tape was used to hold signs together at the clearance event (the horror!).

One time, we walked in to check on a high-end store, and we saw that someone had used a red sharpie marker to create a sign by hand. The information on the sign might have been correct, but the way it was presented did not line up with the brand. The store employees didn't even think they did anything wrong! The store followed directions in terms of displaying the correct information—pursuing this higher-level why—but they didn't do it in a way that resonated with the brand.

There's a delicate balance that we have to strike in terms of letting store managers run their stores like they own them, but then also putting guard rails in place that clearly explain what's expected from them. We like to encourage managers to have a shopkeeper mentality, but we also want to know that the brand and the shopper experience stays consistent across thousands of stores. A customer should get the same shopping experience regardless of whether they're in Kansas, Connecticut, or Alabama—but how do you do that?

The only way to achieve that shopkeeper mentality is by educating people about where the brand is going and setting expectations to maintain consistent delivery. Those two need to be tightly coupled for people to truly have a shopkeeper mentality where they're able to run their business in a meaningful way that resonates with the community, but also represent the entire brand as a fleet of force.

A Disconnect

Some companies decide to separate the brand engagement from the operational information, which creates a disconnect for their workforce. A high-end athletics retailer named Madrone (not their real name) did this during their biggest sneaker launch—which caused some problems. Madrone secured a deal with a star athlete who would represent a pair of their shoes, and millions of dollars were thrown into the marketing campaign, which included social media, print media, and digital media.

But when the stores received the communications for the shoes, the content was so dry and boring that it failed to clearly communicate the importance of the promotion. The communication lacked context, and the stores didn't think it was a big deal. It didn't excite the workforce, it didn't explain the significance of such a partnership, nor did it fully explain what was expected of each store and how important their role was in this promotion.

When a retailer separates brand engagement from the actual operations of bringing it to life in stores, there's a disconnect, and stores don't have the context for proper execution. In Madrone's case, they didn't know that one shoe was tied to a multimillion-dollar marketing campaign and a star athlete—and because its importance wasn't explained or emphasized, the promotion didn't receive the special treatment it should have. Store employees didn't feel compelled to do what needed to be done to bring this product to life.

Employees both want and need to know that their work has value, and that they are not just putting up another piece of marketing. They need to know that the work they do supports the strategy of the entire organization, and they are part of a collective effort (which involves every other store) that is designed to provide maximum satisfaction for the customer. Madrone should have emphasized the link between the employee and the company, as well as between the company and the customer.

WHAT'S THE PROBLEM?

Executive teams are skilled at accurately painting the overall vision of their company. They deliver instructions about tactics, like putting up marketing, changing outfit displays, or swapping mannequins. Even if the overall vision of a company is effectively communicated, however, it isn't always relatable to regular employees.

Executives fall short in giving employees context about their work, creating a disconnect between the employees doing the work and how their efforts tie into the aspirations of the company. Why should an employee feel empowered to put up marketing if they are not being shown how their work impacts the bigger picture?

Disempowered employees become disengaged, which is

happening all too frequently in the retail industry. They lack a connection to the company because they are not given the relevant context as to why their work matters. Even if they carry out individual tasks well, they don't have specific and engaging information that shows them how their efforts contribute to the greater whole.

STEPS TO EMPOWER YOUR WORKFORCE

There are many levels to empowering a workforce. Firstly, retailers should give meaning to the work that individual employees do for the company. To do this, they should provide the information people need to make good decisions, and help them understand how those decisions affect the overall vision of the organization. Employees will feel motivated to know that their work can make an impact and implement change.

A feedback loop can be pivotal in helping employees feel empowered. Associates feed information to marketing collaterals, who speak to district managers, who discuss with corporate. If that loop is followed full circle, people will feel like their voice is valuable and their opinions can help advance the organization.

In turn, this improves employee morale. Every person who works for an organization can act as a marketing vehicle for that organization. Say a company launches an exciting new product line, for example, in which they have partnered with a socially sustainable manufacturer in Guatemala. The first people who need to get on board with the line are the 50,000 associates who work for the retailer. The more excited they are, the more likely they will tell other people about the new line. Inspiration isn't something money can buy, but it is infinitely valuable for retail employees to feel proud to be part of a company. The business benefits because those associates will feel empowered to promote the brand.

Connect the Dots

Everyone wants to make a difference and have autonomy over their work. If you don't see the context of what you're doing, however, you don't even know what you're making a difference for. As a retailer, you should connect the dots between the how and the why of each employee task.

The quality of people's business decisions depends on the amount of context they are given. If people see the business holistically, they can make better judgment calls on how to advance the overall brand (no handmade signs with red sharpies, for example). If they can't see where they are going, they cannot take the right steps to get there. We tell retailers not to separate the information people need to know from the instructions for what they need to do because the two are intricately linked.

People can only act accordingly if they know what is being expected of them and why it's going to make a difference for the overall company. They need a big picture. First, tell them what they need to know about the program, initiative, or best practice. Next, tell them what they need to do (and be sure the expectations are clear!). Lastly, explain why that work matters, how it's going to move the needle for the company, and how their efforts fit into the overall company strategy. The employee will feel like he's needed (because he is), and when people feel needed and important, they feel empowered to get the job done.

Keep the Customer in Mind

Empowering your workers in a way that they feel proud of their role will spill over to excellent customer service, which is something we as retailers aim to offer.

One company that provides excellent customer experience is Kwik Trip, a gas station chain located in the Midwest. That's right! A gas station!

Kwik Trip has grown as a company because of their impressive customer service. Not only are the employees friendly, helpful, and engaging, but they are also fast, providing the customer with what they need. The staff understand the role they play in the overall vision of the brand. The CEO also knows that in order to remain competitive with other retailers that might sound more appealing, he has to offer a competitive hourly salary. Not only are his employees being paid more than average, but the message is that the company cares about its employees and as such, employees are loyal to the brand. Gas stations might not typically be known for customer service, but this company has found great success. Their efficiency and quality customer service—due to their empowerment—helps drive the business.

Another brand that focuses on customer experience is Lululemon. In each of their store locations, Lululemon works to create a sense of community. They have opened yoga shops and set up tea bars inside their stores, for example. They are providing their customers with a unique experience they wouldn't be able to get anywhere else. Not only do they consistently satisfy customers nationwide, but they also offer localized experiences. The store managers and associates make good judgment calls about adding local flavor to stores. Austin, for example, has a great personality as a city. The Lululemon stores in Austin focus on reflecting the city's personality authentically in that store environment.

Being an associate in a company typically means being in a sales position. The associates are in charge of increasing the size of each customer's basket and driving the brand loyalty. Lululemon takes a different approach. They call their associates educators. When we spoke to someone who used to work for the company, she mentioned she never liked being considered a salesperson. It was much more effective for her to think of her job in terms of education. She saw more value in teaching people about healthy living, yoga, and running than simply selling products. She felt far more empowered knowing she could help change people's lives rather than get money from their wallets.

These team members were still technically associates in that they generated sales and drove the business forward. However, calling them educators gave them a greater sense of connection with the customer and the overall brand vision. It was transformative for employees to think of their jobs as being about more than just the money.

Listen to the Front Lines

Never underestimate the importance of listening. If the teams in your stores have something to say, it's crucial you hear it. A big part of making people feel empowered is having them feel heard and understood by those above them.

Store employees have valuable opinions because they are on the front lines. They view the competition and engage with customers every day. They see firsthand what works and what doesn't in regard to both products and customers. Establish working feedback channels so that executives can hear information from those on the front line. Associates should provide feedback to their district managers, who then relay these to corporate.

Communication doesn't end when executives hear feedback, however. Once they have heard and considered employee opinions, retailers should circle back to their teams about how their insights have changed the course of the company or impacted business decisions. Communicating back to the associates or store managers is important to reassure them that their voice is being heard.

There are various ways for a company to collect feedback. One method is conducting surveys. Keeping an open channel for communication is another, similar to the dialogue, discussion, and debate channels like Slack. A third is an associate-friendly app. Platforms like this not only allow store associates to communicate with each other, but with corporate executives as well.

Some companies use more traditional methods, like actually calling the store team to ask for feedback about a new product, for example. The point is that *all* anecdotal feedback can help executive teams make future decisions and implement changes. However, because it is time consuming to call each and every store, technology can help retailers streamline and synthesize the key themes from feedback.

Equip Employees with the Right Tools

We often hear that associates in stores are nervous to approach, help, or socialize with customers. Younger employees feel especially intimidated to walk up to a customer who probably has more information and experience than them. While the employee is engaging with the customer, the latter is telling them more about the product or the terms and conditions of a sale than the employee knows themselves.

Equipping your team with the right tools means giving them enough information to know how they can feel helpful when it comes to interacting with customers. Help them become educators, making each customer experience more than a transaction.

Let's say it's the holiday season and a customer walks into a store looking for a Christmas present for a family member. A properly equipped and empowered employee will start a friendly and productive conversation with that customer to help them find the right gift. They might ask where the family member lives and look up the trending gift items in that area. They would find out the customer's price point and direct them toward a certain area of the store, giving targeted recommendations based on how much the customer is willing to spend. Business owners should curate information in order for associates to feel more empowered to give their customers better retail experiences.

Engage and Inspire

The key to moving 50,000 people in a single, unified company direction is to engage and inspire them as much as possible. Remember that people in retail choose where they want to work. The minimum-wage employees are especially important to motivate, because their salary is the same whether they work for one retailer or another. Make them identify with *you* and want to be loyal to *your* company by giving them the relevant information to feel like part of the brand.

Ask yourself what type of employer you want to be. Rally people behind you and your brand. If you know that your associates are inspired by Beyoncé, and she happens to walk into one of your stores, make sure you share that with them so that they can feel like part of a larger community. Your goal is to make them feel proud of big brand moments.

Just like there is a promise between a brand and its customers, there should also be a promise between a brand and its employees. The happier your employees, the longer they'll want to work for you, and the better customer service they'll be motivated to provide.

Employees should be exposed to the same information about the brand as its customers are. There are various ways for them to receive this live information: either through an app, social media feed, or text notifications. How they receive the information isn't as important as making sure that they actually have the same access and visibility to the brand posts as the customers. They should be watching the same videos and reading the same Facebook posts. That way, if a customer walks into a store and mentions they have seen a pair of pants on social media, the employee will know exactly what they are talking about. This establishes more of an emotional connection between the employee and the customer, which provides both with greater satisfaction.

Associates are a vital part of your business. They are typically younger, which means they are more exposed to consumer technology. They want to be shown, not told, about how things work. This audience benefits from funny videos and images. Communication today is different from what it was like two, five, and ten years ago. In today's society, we use GIFs, emoticons, texts, and memes to connect with others. Companies have to adapt to these modes of communication if they want to retain modern customers and employees. If an employer has a sixteen-year-old employee, they need to engage with that employee in a way that will be relevant to them. We as retailers must use their language and adopt the necessary technologies to interact with different age groups.

When looking to inspire your team, think outside of the box. Your employee is simultaneously your customer and your best advocate. There are so many original and effective ways for employers to converse with their employees and encourage them to participate in the overall brand philosophy.

The same campaigns companies would design to engage customers can work for their employees. Retailers have thousands of associates who need to feel as motivated as possible to do their job well. In the past, we've created internal videos interviewing merchants about new product lines, or having product designers talk about the latest trends in stores. This gets employees excited about promoting and selling to customers.

Guerrilla marketing is an advertisement strategy in which businesses promote their products in an unconventional way. This could involve sending out promotional surprise coupons, scratchers, or adventure trips to your associates. In the past, we've made cookies or origami figures with details about the new product on the back. We've designed tablecloths people can draw on and word puzzles they can fill out. Although these ideas seem random, they are fun and effective ways to get employees engaged.

Inspired associates understand the value of the different promotions being run and recognize their own contribution to making these promotions happen. The more empowered employees feel, the easier it is to collect accurate information from them. Retailers need to collect data from across their retail footprint in order to measure the successes and shortcomings of their business.

Sometimes associates will notice trends faster than headquarters will. Sometimes it's the opposite. Either way, it's important to establish a two-way communication channel where each side can feed information back to the other. Both quantitative and qualitative feedback is important for measuring business results and figuring out the next steps a business should take.

It isn't enough for a retail business to create a brand strategy and know how to speak about it. It is far more important for a business to engage its people in that strategy. Individual employees will not feel motivated to participate in campaigns if they don't see the context of why their efforts matter. Inspire your team so they feel like the work they do every day makes a difference.

The more invested your people feel, the more accountability they will have for their tasks, which makes measuring business execution much easier, which we'll cover in the next chapter.

KEY TAKEAWAYS

- Retailers should connect the how and the why for their employees so the latter know that their work is making an impact.

- Understanding the "why" of work leads to better decision making, which drives a business forward.

- The more you engage your employees, the prouder they will feel to work for you, and the more likely they will be to spread positive words about your company.

- Arm each of your employees with the tools they need to effectively execute their tasks.

- Be creative and original when it comes to inspiring your employees.

Chapter 6

PRINCIPLE 5: MEASURE THE EXECUTION

THE FIFTH PRINCIPLE IS THE CAPSTONE to the previous four. Once principles one through four have been successfully implemented, retailers can develop an understanding of whether they are working and making a difference. The quality of in-store execution is what gives businesses their competitive advantage. The more attention a business pays to in-store execution, the better chance it has of succeeding.

To measure the execution of a business, it is critical for executives to pay close attention to the numbers—meaning the data coming out of their stores. They should be capable of analyzing engagement reports and making sense of team feedback to question whether the first four principles are working. And if something isn't working, then they know what to change.

Unfortunately, in our experience, most retailers don't have a way to measure their execution. We ask questions like "What does your execution look like?" and "What percent of the time are tasks completed when you instruct your stores to do them?" The answers we typically get are estimations or guesses based on what their store visits look like; there is no concrete number.

The problem we see most retailers face is getting to that number, which to some seems next to impossible. We get it: you don't know what you don't know. Unless retailers are measuring and paying attention to whether all the different directives, promotions, sales, and events planned for the year were executed—and then understanding what those percentages mean—few retailers have a handle on what their execution rate is. And even if they knew the numbers, they probably wouldn't know what to do with them.

As an industry, retail is also people heavy, not data heavy. People's personalities, opinions, and relationships play a large role in in-store operations.

An example of a company with particularly strong and effective execution is Amazon. As a member of the tech industry, Amazon rigorously watches its business, paying close attention to the numbers. The decision process is a careful one. First, the executives make decisions based on their numbers. Next, they track the outcomes of those decisions. Those outcomes dictate their future decisions. It is a well-oiled iteration process.

This is a common process for software, manufacturing, and

technology industries, and we think it also works well in a retail environment. Historically, the retail industry has thrived off of qualitative feedback. The quantitative figures can be helpful in determining accountability and tightening up store execution.

Because most retailers don't have a system in place to track executions across all stores (and all at once), retailers don't necessarily know what's possible.

Let's take the case of Banner Peak (we changed the name). They've spent millions of dollars and months of work on a mobile POS rollout, and they expected all stores to execute the directives in a timely fashion. This rollout depended on regular store employees, who in addition to this massive project also have their regular store management life to focus on, like making sure customers are taken care of and the like. Maybe Josh in Store 128 broke up with his girlfriend and found it hard to concentrate the week the rollout was being pushed. While Store 129 initiated the rollout with few to no hiccups, Store 128 struggled to meet the milestones, but how does Banner Peak's IT department know what's happening across their stores? Well, they did what all retailers have done for years and years: Banner Peak's IT department spent weeks calling each store, waiting on hold, looking for managers, and simply asking whether the rollout was implemented or not. They also conducted some in-store visits to check on progress.

This isn't to say this is the wrong way of tracking execution. It's simply the way it's been done—but with today's technology, there's a much more effective way to measure execution across all stores.

At Zipline, we believe in data, and we believe in seeing that data first thing every morning, whether it lands in your mailbox or you log in to your Roll Up report. There are two sets of numbers that drive business: sales and execution. Understanding those two in tandem can really help structure and propel your business forward. As such, we believe that these critical numbers should be accessible to the people who are responsible for driving the business. They help you get a sense of where your business is at, which helps you become a more efficient retail organization. We helped Banner Peak measure their execution, and the entire IT department was ecstatic because now they knew the status of everything every morning instead of having to chase each store down for a verbal update.

We've been measuring the execution for another retailer, and they reported that with Zipline, they've stepped up their execution from 20 percent to over 90 percent. They're not only able to measure their execution, but they're able to see significant improvement in business because they have a lot more control over the levers in their stores, their inventory sale-throughs, their markdowns, and so on.

HOLD PEOPLE ACCOUNTABLE

It's hard to measure anything, let alone execution, if systems aren't in place to hold people accountable. Unfortunately, lack of accountability is quite common in retail. If managers claim they missed a memo, it's almost impossible to hold people accountable for their actions, and their excuses are translated into shortcomings for the entire organization. People like to blame technology or mis-leading instructions to avoid accepting responsibility (tsk, tsk).

Retailers are responsible for putting systems in place to hold people accountable. If a store receives one thousand emails per week from various departments, it is difficult to determine which messages are most important. A store manager can hardly be blamed if an email gets sent directly to their spam folder. However, this doesn't take away from the problem: companies can't hold their people accountable for the information they read or receive. (Implementing the first four principles should drastically reduce this problem. If this is still a prevalent problem among your stores, we suggest you revisit and alter principle two: establishing intent-based communication.)

Any organization that uses a single-directional technol-ogy without a feedback loop will struggle with the question of accountability. We know of a specialty clothing retailer that still faxes their stores information, for example. We're not kidding. Faxing information moves in one direction only, and there is no room for feedback. Who should be held accountable if the fax sheet falls off the fax machine and slides under the desk? What if a fax machine in a store in the Midwest is broken? What if no one notices the fax machine is broken because...well...because who uses fax machines anymore? With this method and others like it, headquarters cannot see who received and read important notices. We call this a *post-and-pray method*: employers send out communications or introduce initiatives and then hope for the best. Hoping that your teams receive relevant information isn't a viable business strategy.

We emphasize accountability in retail for a number of reasons. First, store teams rotate. With constantly changing staff, it is difficult to know who has done what. This is especially concerning if the work is not up to standard. If the manager doesn't know who did the work, how can she even attempt to fix the problem? Second, workforces are distributed over various locations. There isn't an effective way for retailers to gain visibility into every one of their stores.

THE DATA SIDE OF MEASURING

To properly measure execution, a retailer needs to consider its stores, know which stores executed properly and which didn't, and have clear access to that data to analyze. This type of data will allow retailers to understand the breadth of where execution isn't happening, so then they can do something about it.

Data can tell you whether people are doing the work they are supposed to be doing. Are tasks being completed to move the business forward? Instead of hoping and praying, retailers can gather meaningful and relevant information. The more data retailers have, the better equipped they are to make course corrections for initiatives and to ensure successful outcomes. It's up to us as retailers to decide which information is meaningful and relevant.

Say a company sends out a marketing communication to their stores that involves fifteen steps to complete the implementation. The retailer needs to know which stores are getting it done and which ones are falling behind. Some stores may be performing better than others. Why? By measuring such data, executives can get a sense of these successes and failures across the whole spectrum of their business. If an entire region is falling behind, for example, the data can point to a possible explanation. Perhaps the problem was that the region hadn't received the relevant information. Maybe there was an issue with shipping, or the distribution center might not have had the right products in stock. Tracking this information offers data for executives to act on.

As soon as the root cause of an issue is identified, a company can think about the areas they should target. Maybe they need to check in with a specific store or contact the distribution center. The data drives the feedback loop, and vice versa. The goal of the fifth principle is for employers to see whether the work gets done, check if the work is up to standard, and plan a conversation if it isn't.

It is valuable to question which pieces of data are important. It might not be crucial to immediately know which people have read notices, for example. Maybe it is and that's something that is important to the CEO. At Zipline, we find it important to know if stores check tasks off, raise any concerns, or report missing critical marketing materials.

Maximize Visibility

After figuring out which data is critical for you, the next step is to make that data visible. Your entire organization will benefit from access to relevant data. Stores need to be able to see where they are in the rollout. District managers should have a good sense about where their stores are and what role they have in the rollout, as this helps maintain that alignment from principle one. If every level of a business can see where it stands, they will be able to make decisions and take actions that will remain in line with the rest of the company.

When we talk about measuring execution and gathering data, what we essentially mean is clarifying what people are being asked to do and getting insight on whether or not it is done. Only once a retailer has that clarity and insight can they make an educated decision about moving forward.

For example, often retailers test products to inform their buys for next season. They are experimenting to see what resonates best with customers. If a graphic t-shirt sells particularly well, merchants will specifically call stores to make sure those t-shirts are displayed loudly.

The easier people receive information, the more aligned people will be about the test. The merchant, store team, and district managers will all be on the same page about when the test units will be delivered, how they should be merchandised, how long they should be on the floor, what the expectations for selling are, and what the specific selling points are for customers. People can only make informed decisions if they actually have access to the right information.

If there is additional work a person can do, they should be made aware of this. Employees feel empowered if they are able to help with specific initiatives. They won't be able to help, however, if they don't have access to the information which explains that initiative.

Make your initiatives easy to visualize and actionable. Retailers could create a *heat map* of the organization and mark red areas which would benefit from extra work. Heat maps are an effective way to look at large amounts of data, as they show entire cohorts which seem to be in trouble. Companies could also create callouts for individual stores or regions which need help. Whichever strategy is adopted, it should pull an initiative to the forefront and make people want to work on it by showing them the specific steps to do so.

The current problem is that chaos beats visibility, and the right information isn't easily accessible. Another contributor to the problem is the archaic way in which retailers receive information. Often the data is arranged into Excel or CFB. It is becoming a lot easier for people to visualize data and follow trends in unconventional ways. A heat map is a good visual, for example. We've seen retailers use pictures of the United States with images bubbled up to indicate marketing issues. Retailers should think outside of the box when it comes to presenting data visually, as it will improve the visibility and clarity of information.

Data clarity is crucial in determining the success of a business initiative. Imagine a company is running a pilot marketing campaign, and they instruct half of their stores to implement the campaign and the other half not to. The executive team wants to measure the sales and foot traffic data from all of their stores. When analyzing these numbers, they will assume that those stores which were asked to implement the campaign did, and those which were asked not to did not.

Throughout the test, there will likely be individual stores

that fail to implement the campaign, despite being asked to. If a retailer sees this in time, they can exclude these stores from the overall analysis and still use the real and accurate data to make decisions about the business. Say a company is doing a point-of-sale rollout, for example. When analyzing the data, the retailer decides the rollout is successful because they notice an uptake in sales and a decrease in technical support and technical issues.

When field, regional, and district managers are working with accurate and physical data, they can have much stronger conversations with employees about accountability. If managers do visit stores, they can easily identify red areas and discuss tasks that were marked as completed but were not, for example. It is no longer a theoretical conversation about improving execution, but a practical one. Managers can engage in much more effective team development when they can see and work with the relevant data, as they can know which actions stores did and didn't carry out.

THE PROCESS SIDE OF MEASURING

From a process standpoint, companies need to set standards. Just because a task is executed doesn't mean it is executed well. If there is a clear expectation as to how work should be carried out, it becomes much easier to evaluate how well stores are carrying out their tasks. Companies could set execution to a scale, for example, and measure thousands of locations at a time according to that scale.

Technology

Technology that can provide retailers with all the feedback and data they need to measure execution and take action currently exists. The most appropriate technology depends on which information is most meaningful to retailers.

In our experience, the majority of retailers are interested in the execution and compliance across stores. They want to see how individual stores or clusters of stores carry out the tasks they were instructed to complete. Retailers also want to separate the data into the specific initiative that was launched, how this was executed, and how the initiative is performing.

The initiative could be a technology rollout, marketing campaign, or annual performance review. The first step is to gather and analyze the information on an initiative and a store level. The second step is to set up technology that'll help retailers track the behavior on both of those levels. This technology should allow for appropriate accountability. If the fitting room fixtures were done wrong, but the employer doesn't know who carried out the task, they cannot have a conversation about how to improve for next time.

How to Use Technology Wisely

Technology helps filter information and produce visual reports, which give retailers a real- time pulse on the work that is being carried out. It provides a consistent stream of data about the actions happening in each store so retailers no longer have to call hundreds of stores to ask if tasks were executed. When retailers receive this information in real time, they can work to pivot and adjust any initiatives that are not succeeding.

Real-time notifications and dashboards allow a retailer to notice the moment a store falls behind. In the past, businesses would use analytics tools or pool their data in Excel and receive a report six weeks later. Thanks to today's incredible advancements, we can receive real-time data that will allow for fast and targeted business decisions.

Nowadays, technology can gauge time in a way that wasn't possible before. Task management systems, for example, can track a person's individual tasks, when they were completed, and how long it took them. With this data, retailers get a new perspective on the workload and execution that stores can support at an individual level. They are no longer estimating how long tasks will take their stores.

Not only can retailers get an idea as to how long tasks take in each store, but they can compare performances between stores. For example, a store in one city might be able to get their marketing displays up in thirty minutes, while another store might take three hours. What happened there? With this data, they can see accountability at a granular, individual-store level. Why did the second store take longer? What can be done to fix this?

We recommend retailers focus on the specifics within the task management tools. Understand the workloads in the context of each individual store. Once you do, you can allocate labor appropriately, based on the workload necessary for specific tasks in specific stores.

Measuring Individuals

Technology can help retailers examine individual performance and store performance. Comparing this data allows retailers to identify overall trends and behavior and notice the outliers that aren't performing to the best of their ability.

Whichever technology you choose, we recommend choosing one that allows you to give each member of the organization a unique identity. These technologies should pave the way for retailers and employers to have productive conversations with their teams about accountability, growth, and opportunity.

Individualized technologies mean retailers can ask questions that will provide them with better information. The next step is to arrange that information in such a way that it can be analyzed and acted on.

Say a retailer wants to ask 50,000 store employees about their favorite product of the summer or whether they have any suggestions about the product line. These questions aren't designed for multiple choice answers, but the retailer doesn't want to have to read through 50,000 written answers either. Although this is qualitative data, it should be actionable and digestible for executives who are too busy to spend a lot of time reading and analyzing information. This is where the right technology is crucial.

THE HEALTH SCORE

We advocate for retailers to make good use of a health score. Employers cannot accurately predict the likelihood that a task will get executed in their company stores. Many guess this likelihood based on the store's previous behavior and execution history. This makes up the health score of a store.

For example, one region might have a health score of 60 percent, which means there is a 60 percent chance that they will execute a task on time and correctly in that area. Another region might have a health score of 99 percent. These health scores can help retailers understand where to direct their executive leadership, training, and monitoring. It can help pinpoint the areas in which a business needs to improve to bring their total organization up to 100 percent.

PAIRING YOUR SYSTEMS

When you pair a learning management system (LMS) with a task management system, you can determine which employees are getting tasks done and which employees know the products best. Because these systems help identify performance, they can match people together so they can work more effectively as a team.

For example, a store manager observes their team and realizes Sarah has great product knowledge and Jack is effective at getting tasks done, but he lacks product knowledge. The manager could decide to pair these two up. Jack can help Sarah improve at getting things done, and Sarah can help Jack with product knowledge.

In this way, a store manager can identify where the bright spots are in their workforce. Furthermore, a regional director or an HR training manager can see who warrants a promotion throughout the organization. They can identify which employees are thriving and consider them for training, learning sessions, and corporate opportunities. Not only can the high performers be identified and rewarded, but they can be guided toward further growth.

Task and learning management systems can provide clear, actionable tracking of individual employees that can help improve and drive the business as a whole.

PHOTOGRAPHIC EVIDENCE

Some retailers are now encouraging their stores to take pictures of their marketing displays. First, this allows retailers to verify whether or not the displays were set up. Second, retailers can identify whether or not the displays were set up properly. Photos confirm if the task was done and if it was done well.

What if a retailer has 1,500 stores worldwide and each has a different floor plan? It sounds pretty unrealistic to scroll through thousands of photos to confirm that every store has successfully set up a marketing display. If only there were a system that could automatically compare those photos and immediately highlight the outliers.

Well, we're in luck! Because there is! Using a task management system can highlight the outliers and make it less time consuming for retailers to judge their in-store execution. On top of this, if stores are unsure about the type of picture they need to take, a task manager can both provide an example of the picture and map out what the actual display should look like. Yay, technology!

If you establish a link between task management and feedback reporting, you can annotate the outlier photos and send them back to stores. With the visual feedback, stores can see exactly what needs to be fixed. This feedback loop helps maintain consistency across stores.

CAN EXCEL BE VALUABLE?

Although old school, Excel shouldn't be disregarded altogether. Excel *can* still be valuable for automatically arranging data.

Say a retailer is looking at two weeks' worth of data for the task completion in their stores. On the spreadsheet, the rows represent the stores, the columns represent the days, and each square has the task completion rate for that store on that day. Green is for high values and red is for low values. In Excel, the whole sheet can colorize itself based on which values are closer to green and which are closer to red. If 100 is the highest, a row with 95, 92, 97, and 98 will easily come up green.

In this instance, the stores with lower values can be easily identified. If a store has 0, 7, 9, and 20, it is clear that this store is struggling. Not only can the low-performing stores be identified, but the colors can help employers track patterns. If a store was green and suddenly became red, a retailer could pinpoint the store and question the lack of task completion. Perhaps a store manager left or was replaced.

The data to generate this Excel spreadsheet comes from a task managing tool. Other data obtained from task managing tools could include the readership of communication across all of a company's stores, the time it took to read a communication, or the time it took to implement a marketing rollout.

REPORTING TO HEADQUARTERS

Stores are a critical part of the company chain because they are the ones carrying out the tasks; they are the end product. However, without a complete loop in which information gets reported back to headquarters, it is impossible for executives to understand the capabilities of each store and determine their workloads.

If a marketing executive sends information to thousands of stores and notices that 15 percent of the stores report they haven't received the marketing, a feedback loop would help identify the similarities between those stores that failed to receive the marketing. The issue could be due to a particular distribution center, which never sent the window posters out. This becomes a headquarters problem.

We often see retailers asking for insight into the information that different business partners are sending to stores. Headquarters should have an understanding of how many communications the visual department is sending compared to marketing and compared to IT, as this helps to determine people's workloads.

Every department, including inventory, finance, merchandising, marketing, and loss prevention, all have an end goal, which usually comes down to stores completing their tasks. In the retail industry, stores are at the finish line because that's where consumer transactions take place. While each department sends tasks to stores, there are only two people to direct the traffic and plan the work so that stores can get it done.

BE CONSISTENT

Consistency breeds good habits. To create consistency in a company, give people access to data and establish a working feedback loop. Technology provides companies with a consistent flow of data, which can help stores move towards better habits, and help headquarters move in a bigger and better direction. The more visible this information, the better people can understand where they are at in terms of business, and the more they can determine where things are going wrong. The consistent feedback loop drives the organization forward.

RINSE AND REPEAT

If a business implements the first four principles, the fifth justifies the hard work because it gives the company an opportunity to see if its work paid off. Whether it did or didn't, there are always opportunities for improvement.

When you measure the execution of a business, you can identify areas that need more work. The fifth principle reminds business owners to pay attention to what they've already done and to what they're going to do. These principles aren't one-and-done principles either. The retail business is a moving target, and as such, all of these principles should be revisited, adjusted, and once you feel you've nailed it, consistent. Your communication isn't automatically successful if you send a couple of real-time messages. Most of our principles take a great deal of trial and error until you find what works specifically for you and your unique situation. Measuring your execution should remind you that, if a piece of the puzzle is missing, you should go and find it.

The retail business is always evolving. Once these principles are in place, you should be refining them. A business owner should constantly be checking that their business is progressing in the right direction. Check to make sure your organization is still aligned. Question if your communication is as intent based as possible. Track the improvement of your business according to your new initiatives. Is the right message being sent at the right time? If it isn't getting better, ask yourself what needs to change and take the necessary steps to drive improvement.

Each one of the principles heavily relies on technology. The key to an aligned organization is visibility, which involves well-implemented tools. Intent-based and real-time communication relies on specific channels.

Every member of a successful business should be on board with what has been done, what needs to be done, and who should be held accountable for these tasks. You'll never be able to move forward if everyone is on a different page.

The fifth principle is a natural progression from the other four. When you measure the execution, you can see if they've worked or not. The more visible the data, the better retailers can track accountability. Measuring execution depends heavily on having a working feedback loop in which headquarters can identify execution on a store and regional level. As with the other principles, the right technology drives a retailer's ability to measure data. Pick individualized methods that recognize the uniqueness of your employees.

Measuring the execution might be the last of the principles, but it is certainly not the least if a retailer is interested in knowing whether their hard work was worth it.

KEY TAKEAWAYS

- Communicate effectively to find out if people are doing the work they are being asked to do.

- Maximize visibility of data to hold people accountable for tasks.

- Use the data to identify trends and patterns. If something is successful, take note and repeat. If something isn't working, identify what and where to take relevant action.

- Get feedback in a way that is meaningful and accurate. Close the feedback loop to get the entire company on the same page.

- Test, learn, test, learn, test, learn to constantly evolve and grow your business.

CONCLUSION

IN MARKETING AND ADVERTISING, it used to be that 50 percent of a company's spending was ineffective. While half of their initiatives would work, the other half would fail because the company wasn't clear about the intent of the advertising or where it was going. Companies couldn't accurately track the effects of their ad spend or effectively target audiences and adjust their message.

Thankfully, that is no longer the case for marketing and advertising, and it doesn't have to be true for retail either.

With modern technology, we have all this information at our fingertips. Our five principles are specifically designed to work together, each one building off of the one before it. Taking one of them and applying it isn't likely to make much of a difference, but when implemented the way they're intended, vast improvement will follow.

In order to compete in today's business world, retailers are trying to change the trajectory of their business. They want to turn around and drive their business higher and faster by increasing customer loyalty and sales.

In retail, communication is the conduit for success. The outcomes for which we strive as retailers can be achieved through proper and effective communication. Improving communication dramatically improves all of our lives. The better people understand what their role is, the better they feel. Inspire your employees by giving them clarity. That way, they will feel engaged to provide better retail experiences for your customers.

Ineffective communication takes its toll on retail businesses. It does nothing but create confusion, suffering, and struggle in the organization, which leads to frustration, lethargy, and cynicism. Employees feel disengaged, which negatively impacts the brand as a whole.

Retail is designed to provide good service to customers. To better our in-store experiences, we need to focus on clarifying our priorities and driving higher brand engagements by clearing up communication.

WHERE SHOULD YOU BEGIN?

We as retailers need to think ahead. Ask yourself what you want to accomplish in the next year. In the next five? What are your top priorities in running your business? How can each of the five principles apply to your top priorities? Is your organization aligned? Are you communicating with intent in the right places? Are you sending the right messages to the right audiences at the right time? How can you better empower your workforce? Do you know your current execution?

After you have identified your priorities and what you most want to change in your organization, it's time to get your team on board. Do they know where the company is headed? Do people understand their priorities? Do they know their individual role in implementing changes successfully?

Do your salespeople know where to go to get the right information? Can they navigate different vehicles and chat portals? Are they clear on how to access their day-to-day responsibilities?

A disengaged workforce can be disastrous for a business. Are you providing the right tools to inspire people to do their jobs? Are you effectively rallying your employees behind you and your business changes?

Do you have the proper measurement tools in place in order to measure the execution of the five principles? Do you have the right metrics to determine whether your initiatives are working?

The more questions you ask, the more productive conversations you can have with your employees. These conversations can act as a kick-starter for your teams to take action and drive the business forward.

YOU ARE NOT ALONE

As retailers, we know it isn't easy to win customers while sales are declining. We are all too familiar with the struggles in a highly competitive environment. We, too, implemented rollouts and initiatives that failed in the past, unclear of how to make them successful.

We've been there. You are not alone.

Too many retailers feel like they are the only ones facing communication problems. We've spoken to business owners who feel like no one understands how much their organization is changing and how much pressure is on their stores.

Whatever your challenges, we have likely been through them too. Throughout our own trials and errors, that's how we've created the principles and the order in which to implement them. With these foundations in place, not only have other actions become easier, but we can now accurately measure the success of our retail execution. Every action can now be analyzed from a data perspective, from rolling out a mobile POS to implementing a new outfit strategy to experimenting with a store case.

We hope you use this book as a guide to get started. We want this book to be a resource you can use to better your business, both in terms of communication and sales. It wasn't designed to teach you how to be a specific type of business; that's up to you. Whatever your brand vision might be, however, we know it can be achieved better, faster, and more credibly with better communication. Our mission is to improve the lives of a million retail employees by 2020.

The second you gain control over and visibility into your execution, you can start increasing your sales. When you analyze your data, you are able to identify the areas that need improvement and work on them in a much easier and clearer way. From an operational perspective, this means that every store can focus on satisfying the customer.

Following these principles will help business owners become

less stressed out, as they will see their numbers increasing, their teams coordinating and communicating better, and their rollouts happening ahead of schedule rather than behind it.

While you might feel like the only one fighting an execution battle, not only are your problems common, but there are ways to address and solve these problems. Throughout the book, we have given you examples of the different challenges retailers face, and the steps they take to overcome these obstacles. We hope that you find these relatable and helpful to overcoming your own.

CONNECT WITH US

Improving communication enhances company performance. However, it also impacts people's lives, including our own. Connect with us! We would love to hear from you. We want to hear your struggles and give you targeted advice. We also want to hear your successes and celebrations. We would love for more retailers to engage in a collective discussion around retail execution and communication.

If you're interested, visit getzipline.com/thebook. Tell us about your process and what's working for you. What are you seeing and experiencing in your business environment that could be useful to share with other retail leaders? If you have any questions about how your organization can benefit from our principles, we'd be happy to answer them.

If you follow each of the five principles in this book, we guarantee that you will see dramatic improvements in your retail business—and we're here to help every step of the way!